SEVEN GATES

OF

RIGHTEOUS KNOWLEDGE

*A Compendium of Spiritual Knowledge and Faith for
the Noahide Movement and All Righteous Gentiles*

by

Rabbi Moshe Weiner,
Jerusalem, Israel

author of

SHEVA MITZVOT HASHEM *and* THE DIVINE CODE,

and

Dr. Michael Schulman

Hebrew-to-English translation assistance by

Rabbi Yosef Schulman

Presented by UNITED NOAHIDE ACADEMIES®

⊷ A project of ASK NOAH INTERNATIONAL ⊶

The non-English words or phrases in this book are transliterated Hebrew. The guttural letters ח and כ are represented by "ch" as in the Scottish word "loch."

ISBN 978-1-7333635-5-6

For information contact:

Michael Schulman, Executive Director
Ask Noah International
P.O. Box 1, Pittsburgh, PA 15230 USA
Email: SevenLaws@asknoah.org

www.asknoah.org

Printed in the United States of America

We thank Laurel Tessmer *for her help with proofreading and graphic design.*

Other publications from Ask Noah International:

Sheva Mizvot Hashem, 2nd ed. (Hebrew)

The Divine Code, 4th ed. (Part I also in Spanish and French)

*To Perfect the World: The Lubavitcher Rebbe's Call
to Teach the Noahide Code to All Mankind* (pub. SIE)

Go(o)d for You: The Divine Code of 7 Noahide Commandments

Prayers, Blessings, Principles of Faith, and Divine Service for Noahides
(English, Dutch, French, Portuguese, Spanish, Russian, Indonesian editions)

Prayers for Noahides: Community Services and Personal Worship

Семь Врат Праведности (*Seven Gates to Righteousness*, Russian ed.)

TABLE OF CONTENTS

PREFACE

In Tractate *Sotah* 10b, and in Midrash, *Genesis Rabbah* ch. 54, the sages explained the verse Genesis 21:33 in the following way:

"[Abraham] planted an *eshel* in Beer-Sheba, and there he proclaimed the Name of God, God of the Universe."

"[Abraham] planted an *eshel* in Beer-Sheba" –
[What is this *eshel*?] Reish Lakish said:
This teaches that he made an orchard and planted in it many types of fine fruit trees [to benefit the wayfarers].
Rabbi Nehemiah said: He built an inn
[for the wayfarers, for lodging, food and drink].

"and there he proclaimed the Name of God, God of the Universe" –
Reish Lakish said: Do not read it as "he proclaimed;" rather, read it as "he caused to call." This teaches that our forefather Abraham caused the Name of the Holy One, blessed be He, to be called by the mouth of every passerby.

How? After [the wayfarers] ate and drank, they stood up to bless Abraham.
He would say to them, "Was it then of *my* food that you ate? You ate from the food of the God of the universe.
[Rather, you should] thank, praise and bless He Who spoke and caused the universe to come into being."

They would ask, "What shall we say?"
He told them, "*Blessed is the God of the universe, from Whose bounty we have eaten.*"
So Abraham taught all people to recognize and call in the Name of God, God of the universe.

Like the orchard and the inn that Abraham established in Beer-Sheba, this book sets out a spiritual and moral path for Gentiles (Non-Jews) desiring to become righteous in God's eyes and to have a closer personal relationship with God, our Creator. The ability to achieve these goals requires access to knowledge of the character traits and attitudes that one should cultivate in order to advance in this path. By entering into the "Seven Gates" that are explained in this book, it is possible for a person to reveal and nurture the "image of God" in which we are created. In response to one's own sincere efforts in this direction, he will be aided and blessed from Above to become a servant of God. Since more and more Gentiles are now searching for spiritual truth and understanding, and personal closeness to God, blessed be He, it is vitally imperative for this knowledge to be widely disseminated in the world.

As evidenced by the various novel approaches to spirituality that have arisen in our modern Internet age, it is inevitable that a person can "miss the mark," or even be misled, if he does not evaluate the information he finds in the light of God's framework for a Gentile's pious behavior. That framework is the Seven Commandments for the Children of Noah (in Hebrew, *Sheva Mitzvot*[1] *B'nai Noach*), which are popularly called the Seven Noahide Laws. Nevertheless, this book does not explain the details of the Noahide Laws. Other works by Rabbi Moshe Weiner – *Sheva Mitzvot HaShem* (in Hebrew) and its English version, *The Divine Code* – fulfill that purpose.[2] Rather, this book is intended to highlight many of the Torah's universal moral teachings. With this knowledge, a person can find the proper way to connect with and reveal the "image of God" that is within himself and reveal the "image of God" that is within others as well.

---

[1] *Mitzvah* (plural: *mitzvot*) is the word in Hebrew for an eternal Divine commandment from the Torah. In the Torah, we find that from the outset, God commanded seven general *mitzvot* for Gentiles (the Children of Noah), followed by 613 detailed *mitzvot* for Jews (the Children of Israel). However, less than 300 of the Jewish *mitzvot* are applicable in modern times, before the Messianic Era.

[2] For a short introduction to the Seven Noahide Laws based on these works, see *Go(o)d for You: The Divine Code of 7 Noahide Commandments*, pub. by Ask Noah International, and available to download from https://asknoah.org.

The present work was inspired by the book *Sefer Ha'Madah (The Book of Knowledge)* by the great venerated Torah scholar, **R**abbi **M**oshe *ben* (son of) **M**aimon (1135-1204 C.E.[3]), also known as Maimonides, or by his acronym **Rambam**. *Sefer Ha'Madah* is the first of the fourteen volumes of his work *Mishneh Torah*, which is his monumental codification of the Oral Torah Law. In it, Maimonides explains the Torah's path to true and proper faith-based knowledge. The essential points of our present book, and indeed much of its text, have been taken from Maimonides' holy words in *Sefer Ha'Madah*. Beyond that, we have added background information and explanations to produce a book meant specifically for those Gentiles who are, or who want to become, righteous in God's eyes.

The reader should be aware that we have not even attempted to include every proper and righteous outlook, character trait, and path in life for Gentiles. However, in a general manner, this book presents the proper views and behaviors for a righteous person of any nationality or culture.

---

[3] "C.E." stands for the Common Era, which is the dating system in common use today. Likewise, "B.C.E." stands for Before the Common Era.

Introduction:

The Image of God Within Every Person

"And God said [to His angels], 'Let us make mankind (Adam) in Our image, after Our likeness. They shall rule over the fish of the sea, the birds of the sky, and over the animal, the whole earth, and every creeping thing that creeps upon the earth.' So God [Himself] created mankind in His image, in the image of God He created him; male and female He created them."[4]

These Biblical verses address the creation and the dominion of mankind. God's *intention* in this is to bring about the perfection and spiritual elevation of mankind, and of the world. These two goals are explained as follows.

Perfection and Elevation of Mankind (*Tikkun Ha'Adam*)

God is singularly unique, and He is not limited in any way. He certainly does not have any type of body, description, or physical or spiritual form.[5] Therefore, it is obvious that the above verses from Genesis cannot be taken to literally mean that a human being (or an angel) can be Divine. Rather, they teach us that just as we know that the Creator is singularly unique and distinct from His physical and spiritual creations, so too, we must know that as a reflection of this, mankind is created unique and distinct from anything else among the spiritually lowest (physical) realm.[6]

How is it that mankind differs from all other created beings? It is in the unique human ability to attain conceptual knowledge and use it in the exercise of free will, as the Torah states: "and you will be *like God, knowing good and bad*."[7] We will now explain how the purpose of

---

[4] Genesis 1:26-27.

[5] See Principle 3 of Maimonides' 13 Principles of Faith, in his *Commentary on the Mishnah* (Introduction to the final chapter of Tractate *Sanhedrin*).

[6] See the explanations of Genesis, ibid., by Sforno and Nachmanides (Rabbi Moshe ben Nachman, or Ramban).

[7] Genesis 3:5.

mankind is to use this knowledge to reveal both the "Godly image" and the "Godly likeness" within each person.

In Biblical Hebrew, which is God's holy language, this unique power of *knowledge* that was given by God to mankind is called *da'at*. With his power of *da'at*, each person is able to understand and relate independently to concepts and situations that are apart from him, and removed from his own physical needs and the necessities of his life.

The nature of every other type of created being was fixed by God. Therefore, those entities cannot "freely choose" anything, nor can their deeds be categorized as "good" or "bad." A human being, on the other hand, can decide how he wishes to act in any given situation. Depending on the deed he chooses, he can either elevate or impair and degrade himself and the world around him.

Mankind is identified as having the "image of God." This includes not only these God-given intellectual powers and abilities, but also mankind's spiritual essence. As the great sage Rabbi Akiva is quoted in the Mishnah:[8] "Beloved is mankind, for they were created in the image [of God]; it is even a greater love that it was *made known* to them that they were created in the image [of God], as it says [Gen. 9:6]: "... for in the image of God He made mankind." By choosing to act in ways that are *like* the revealed benevolent ways of the Creator,[9] a person can rise to the point of bringing out the spiritual "likeness of God" that is within him.

In order to enable a person to elevate himself by exercising the gift of free will, God "wrapped" that spiritual essence in a physical human body. Thus, a person is truly a synthesis of body and soul. For example, a person is similar to an animal in that he needs to eat, drink, sleep, relieve himself, etc. A person does not have the ability to essentially change any functions of this type, because these types of functions stem from the *bodily nature*.

On the other hand, the gift of *free will* gives a person the choice and ability to appoint his God-given spiritual soul as the *primary*

---

[8] *Ethics of the Fathers* 3:14.

[9] The Biblical Hebrew prophets revealed that these ways include kindness, justice, mercy, righteousness, graciousness and humility. Beyond these basic virtues, a person should strive to follow all good ways in which God wants people to act.

motivating force within himself. One who chooses to do this is *wise* and *upright*. He trains himself to place his body and its physical desires as secondary considerations that have importance to him only insofar as they are needed to serve the God-given Divine mission of his soul. This is one of the definitions of a *chassid* (a pious person, in Hebrew). Within this distinction there are many levels, but even a *chassid* at the most basic level merits to receive a reward from God for this piety.[10]

Interestingly, in the verses[11] "And God said, 'Let us make mankind' ... He created them," the Torah uses only one of the sacred Names for God: *E'lohim* (as a singular proper name). While this is a holy Name for God, may He be blessed, in other contexts the Hebrew Scriptures also use this word to refer to created beings that exercise power over others. Thus, we find that angels or ruling government officials,[12] judges,[13] etc., may be referred to as *elohim* (as a plural commonplace noun).[14] For this reason, we find that humans are also collectively called "*elohim*," because they have the ability to rule over the creation and improve it – as it is stated,[15] "They [mankind] shall *rule* over the fish of the sea, the birds of the sky, and over the animal, the whole earth, and every creeping thing that creeps upon the earth." Regarding this, the sages of the Midrash said:[16]

> "... they shall rule *(v'yirdu)* over the fish of the sea, etc." This wording [in Hebrew] means "rule," and it also alternatively means "decline." If a person is worthy [by wisely demonstrating that he is

---

[10] However, this in itself is not the underlying main focus of this book. Maimonides, in *Laws of Kings* 8:11, describes a person who is a "*chassid* of the nations of the world." This is a Gentile who is a *chassid* in the sense of being pious before the One True God, in that he specifically accepts and is careful to observe God's Seven Noahide Commandments as his part in the Torah of Moses. In doing so, he merits to receive a place in the future World to Come.

[11] Genesis 1:26-27.

[12] Ibid., 6:2.

[13] Psalms 82:1.

[14] See Maimonides, *Guide to the Perplexed,* Part 1, ch. 2.

[15] Genesis 1:26.

[16] Quoted by Rashi on Genesis 1:26, from Midrash *Genesis Rabbah* 8:13.

primarily serving as an "image of God," then by right], he may rule over the wild beasts and the domestic animals. If he is not worthy, he becomes inferior before them, and the beast rules over him.

This dominion, which God grants to humans, is not only our physical influence over other creatures (through the means that human intelligence devises), but also our ability to uplift other creatures toward their destined spiritual perfection, by including them as part of the world that mankind can make into a dwelling place for God's Divine Presence *(Shechinah)*. The lesson for us is that if a person does not choose to make this effort, to bring out his personal "image of God" to rule over the animalistic nature within him, he can descend to its level, acting similarly to an animal. Even worse, he can "become inferior before them" – i.e., both the animalistic nature of the world and his own animalistic tendencies will rule over him.

Perfection and Elevation of the World (*Tikkun Ha'Olam*)

The verse mentioned earlier, "they shall rule ...," refers not only to mankind's rulership, but also to mankind's obligation to bring the world to perfection in God's eyes, to the extent of human ability. How is this possible?

In the beginning of God's creating the physical realm, there was a shroud of darkness.[17] There was an absence of physical light, and there was also an inner spiritual darkness – the absence of God's Self-revelation. Mankind's service, starting from the time of God's creation of Adam, the first human being, has been to help prepare the world for the Divine light that will shine in the immanent Messianic Era. In each generation, the efforts in this direction have produced fitting "vessels" *(kelim)* through which righteous people will be able to experience the open revelation of God's Presence in the physical world.[18]

We make the world into a place that is fitting for the revelation of God's Presence through two paths, which correspond in a general way

---

[17] See Genesis 1:2.

[18] This will include the righteous people of all the past generations through the Resurrection of the Dead, which is explained in the last two chapters of this book.

to the verse in Psalms, "Turn away from evil and do good, seek peace and pursue it":[19]

(1) **Establishing societies that are based upon, and operate with, justice and righteousness.** This can be achieved through correct partnerships between people, as the prophet proclaimed:[20] "For thus said God, Creator of the heavens – He is *E'lohim*, the Designer of the earth and its Maker; He established it; not for naught was it created, but rather it was formed to be *settled* – I am God, and there is no other."

(2) **Transforming the world into a more spiritually suitable place by performing acts of goodness and kindness, and by encouraging others to do the same.** Each good deed and each kind act serves as a "vessel" (*keli*) in which God's Presence can dwell in the world.

Therefore, every person, and especially a pious person, should know that by working to perfect and spiritually elevate himself and the world around him, he will follow in the footsteps of Abraham, who called out to all people to recognize God's Name and to fulfill His will through righteous living. Obviously, we cannot specify one outlook and list of traits that will fit the life of every Gentile. Nevertheless, this book does present views and behaviors that are appropriate for a righteous person of any nationality or culture. With this goal, we have identified and set out to explain seven "Gates" for the knowledge and traits of righteous individuals.

May this help to hasten the immanent time when all people will walk in the light of the knowledge of God.

---

[19] Psalms 34:15.
[20] Isaiah 45:18.

THE FIRST GATE: THE GATE OF KNOWLEDGE OF GOD

Chapter 1

RECOGNITION OF GOD'S EXISTENCE AND HIS ESSENTIAL UNITY[21]

The foundation of all proper opinions and all proper traits in a person's behavior, as well as the purpose of all knowledge in general, is the knowledge of God, may He be blessed. Therefore, the first required step in the spiritual ascent of a person is to try to know God.

Drawing Closer to God on a Personal Level

The ultimate mission and greatness of mankind is to gain understanding and knowledge of God, each person according to his own strengths and abilities. In order to achieve this recognition, it is necessary, but not sufficient, for a person to have faith in the principles which the righteous Jewish sages have explained in the past about God. This is based on their chain of tradition from Moses our teacher and the subsequent true prophets of the Hebrew Bible, and through their own Divinely inspired insights. Beyond that, it is the obligation of each person to try to understand such matters with his own intellect, so that he may know them. In this way, a person can come to know and recognize the true existence of God, according to his ability.

This knowledge is not only meant to be an intellectual grasp. It is also an attitude and outlook within the heart and emotions. When a person thoughtfully chooses his actions based on his belief in God, this will also draw his personal character traits in this direction. This happens because it is human nature that exercising the ability to control one's actions will serve to reveal and draw out his heart's desire for the path he is choosing. In this way, he can demonstrate to himself and those around him that recognizing and internalizing Godliness, in addition to desiring it, is within a person's ability.

Nevertheless, it is also an obligation to believe with simple, child-like faith in the Creator and Master of everything, for, as will be

---

[21] This chapter is based on Maimonides, *Laws of the Foundations of Torah*, ch. 1, and 2:9-10. See also *The Divine Code*, Part I, topics 1:1-5.

explained, it is impossible for a person to understand and recognize the Creator completely. Only a small aspect of God's existence can be understood, because it is essentially entirely beyond the grasp of any creation, including even the greatest prophets and the highest angels.

From this it follows that there should be two dimensions to a person's relationship with God. On the one hand, it is incumbent on each person to know and recognize God and His Unity, to the extent of one's ability, with the goal to fill his mind and the emotions of his heart with his understanding of the Creator, and to act according to "the ways of God" (which will be explained further on). At the same time, he should believe that God, may He be blessed, is completely beyond any human being's grasp.

Through achieving a synthesis of these three soul powers – recognition, understanding and belief – and actually expressing them through his thoughts, traits and emotions, a person will more completely cleave to and be attached to the One True God. This will also provide the key for him to tap into levels within his belief and faith that are beyond his knowledge and intelligence. This is the spiritual accomplishment of becoming a *chassid* (a pious person), which is the title of one who is actively attaching himself to the True God, may He be blessed. It is this service which God seeks from a person, and it is this service which draws God to a person.

Explanations from Torah of God's Existence

God's existence is *independent*. That is to say, it is not dependent on anything else, whereas the existence of every creation is dependent on God's will to create it. In the terminology of the sages, this is called God's *Requisite Existence*, which means that there is no cause for His existence. Rather, His existence is essential and due to Himself. His creations, on the other hand, are called *possible existences*, since their existence always depends on another cause, and it is possible that they will either exist or not exist.

Therefore, God's existence is not at all comparable to that of any created thing in the heavens above or the earth below, including time and space and anything that exists within the context of those dimensions. Every creation has limitations to its existence and power and is comprised of multiple parts and elements, be they physical or spiritual. Therefore nothing can be compared to the Holy One, Blessed be He, Who has no limitation to Himself or His power. His power is infinite, endless and unlimited, and His existence is not made up of any combinations. Rather, His existence is a simple Oneness, which has no end and no beginning, and no reason or objective for being.

The unique Truth of the Creator is also elevated and transcendent beyond the truth of the creations. Since a creation is limited and has limited power, what is considered truth in its own context is limited in comparison to the absolute Truth of the Creator. A person can only describe the truth of what he understands and feels, and if something is beyond his comprehension and senses, he cannot know it at all, so certainly, he does not know the whole truth about it. Likewise, what is truth in the estimation of any intellect (be it human or angelic) is limited to what it perceives as truth. The more narrow its ability of knowledge and comprehension, the more limited will be the truth it can conceive of. For example, an adult knows that what a child considers to be an absolute truth it is not the entire truth, but only a portion of it.

Just as God's absolute existence is not comparable to the dependent existence of the creations (because the Holy One, blessed be He, has no *need* whatsoever for them), so too, His absolute Truth is not like their partial truth. This is what the prophet expressed by saying, "The Lord God is True."[22] Likewise, it is written in the Torah, "There is none beside Him."[23] This includes the meaning that there is no other existence that is comparable to Him. Although all the authentic prophets and sages yearned to intellectually know the truth of His existence, it cannot be grasped in its entirety – as it says, "Can you find the comprehension of God? Can you find the ultimate bounds of the Almighty?"[24]

If so, what did Moses, our teacher, want to comprehend when he requested, "Please show me Your glory"?[25] He asked to know the truth of the existence of the Holy One, blessed be He, to the extent that it could be internalized within his mind. By analogy, this is the manner

---

[22] Jeremiah 10:10.

[23] Deuteronomy 4:35.

[24] Job 11:7.

[25] Exodus 33:18.

in which one knows a particular person whose face he saw and whose image has been engraved within his heart; that individual's identity is distinguished within his mind from the identities of others. Similarly, Moses requested that the existence of the Holy One, blessed be He, would be distinguished in his mind from the existence of other entities, to the extent that he would know the truth of God's existence as it is in its own right. Thus, he wished to be granted to understand God on a personal level, and not be dependent on any explanations that would be provided to him. The Holy One, blessed be He, replied to Moses that "man shall not see Me and live."[26] This does not refer to physical sight. Rather, it applies to the insight of the mind's eye, and teaches that it is not within the potential of a living human being (a creature comprised of the synthesis of body and soul) to comprehend Godliness in its essence, separate from any created context. Nevertheless, God revealed to Moses a level of truth of His existence that no other person had known before him, nor would ever know subsequently – as God said,[27] "You [Moses] shall see My back, but you shall not see My face."[28]

This is reflected in the Torah's affirmation, "There has never again arisen a prophet in Israel like Moses."[29] There was a revelation to Moses, our teacher, of an aspect of God's Truth, but it was not the full depth that Moses desired when he made his holy request.

God's Total Incorporeality and Unity

It is clear that the Holy One, blessed be He, is not confined to a body or physical form. Although He may present Himself to a person as a specific form in a prophetic vision, intellectually, that is so the person can receive God's message within his mind and senses. This is the revelation of the Creator through the medium of a certain intellectual context, in accordance with the prophet's level, in order that he will be able to perceive God in some limited way. God can be perceived by one prophet as sitting on a holy throne, or to another as a voice that is

---

[26] Exodus 33:20.

[27] Ibid., 33:23.

[28] See Maimonides, *Laws of the Foundations of Torah* 1:10.

[29] Deuteronomy 34:10.

speaking, and yet these are not true descriptions of God's actual existence, as can readily be understood. Rather, it is a visual or auditory description in the mind, produced by a certain effect that God brings, and this is simply the manner of God's speaking to the prophet or appearing to him in a vision.

Since it has been clarified that God does not have any type of body or corporeal form, it is also clear that none of the functions of a body are appropriate to Him – neither connection nor separation, neither place nor measure, neither ascent nor descent, neither right nor left, neither front nor back, neither standing nor sitting, etc.

God transcends time, so He does not have a beginning, an end, or any age. He does not change, for there is nothing that can cause Him to change. He creates time and space, and those limited dimensions are part of the overall limitations of the universe. But He, in His true existence, is not limited by anything, and therefore He is not under the influence of time and space.

Thus, in regard to all physical descriptions that are related about God in the Hebrew Bible, such as, "He Who sits in the heavens will laugh,"[30] and the like, although it is true that God "does" the said actions, they are not descriptions of His blessed Essence. Rather, they are effects that are brought about in the created spiritual realms by His unified will, and therefore they cause no change in Him. It is in order to inform us of those effects that "the Torah speaks in the language of man;"[31] i.e., the prophets spoke about God using anthropomorphism.

Were He to be angry at times and at other times happy, He would change, and this is not true. As the prophet states: "I, God, have not changed."[32] Rather, all these matters are found in actuality with regard to the created beings. In contrast, He, blessed be He, is infinitely elevated and exalted above all such effects or concepts.

The Holy One, blessed be He, recognizes His truth and knows it as it is. He does not know with a kind of knowledge that is external to Him in the way that we know, for we ourselves and our knowledge are not one and the same entity. Rather, a person is comprised of many faculties, and it is the same with the person's intellect, which acquires

---

[30] Psalms 2:4.

[31] Tractate *Berachot* 31b.

[32] Malachi 3:6.

more knowledge as time passes. The Creator, blessed be He, does not have such categories. His knowledge and His unique life are all one from all aspects and perspectives.

Were He to live as life is humanly conceived, or to know with a knowledge that is separate from Him, there would be many gods: Him, His life, and His knowledge. This is not so. Rather, He is One from all perspectives, in all manners of unity. Thus it is said, "He is the Knower, He is the Known (the Subject of the Knowledge), and He is the Knowledge Itself; all this is One."[33] This matter is beyond the ability of our mouths to relate, or our ears to hear; nor is there the capacity within the heart of a person to grasp it in its entirety.[34]

In reference to a person who knows about some other created entity, there are three divisions: the knower (i.e., the person who knows), the known (i.e., that which is being known about, which is completely separate from the person knowing it), and the knowledge itself (which is extraneous to the person, as it is possible that he will know about the thing, and it is possible that he will not). In contrast, God does not recognize and know the creations in terms of the creations as we know them, but rather He knows them in terms of Himself. Thus, as He knows Himself, He knows every detail of the entire physical and spiritual creation, for the existence of everything created is constantly dependent on Him, as it is His unified will for each thing to be, all as one from its beginning to its end. This is the fact that is expressed by the statement,[35] "I [God] tell the end from the beginning."

---

[33] See Maimonides, *Laws of the Foundations of Torah* 2:10.

[34] Even more, as this is expressed with an anthropomorphic concept of knowledge, it is understood that it only relates to a (high) spiritual level of God's revelation, and not to the essence of God Who is infinitely beyond and separated from any concept of intellect. See *The Gate of Unity and Faith* (*Sha'ar HaYichud Ve'haEmunah*, Tanya, Part II), chs. 8-9, by Rabbi Shneur Zalman.

[35] Isaiah 46:10.

Chapter 2

THE UNITY OF GOD AND HIS POWERS; THE MISTAKEN BELIEF IN INDEPENDENT DEITIES[36]

The sages of the Mishnah taught,[37] "With Ten Utterances, the universe was created," as it says, "In the beginning of God's creating the heavens and the earth, ... God said, 'Let there be light,' ... God said, 'Let there be a firmament in the midst of the waters,' etc."[38] Also, in the Book of Psalms, it says, "Forever, O God, Your word stands firm in the heavens."[39] About these words, Rabbi Israel Baal Shem Tov,[40] o.b.m., explained that God's utterance, "Let there be a firmament, etc.," stands forever in the Heavenly realms and is enclothed in them to give them existence – as it is written, "the word of our God shall stand forever,"[41] and "His words live and stand firm forever."[42] For if the Divine utterance ("Let there be a firmament") would depart from the firmament and return to its source (which is God's power of Divine speech), the Heavenly realms would instantly cease to exist, as if they had never been created, and the creation would be as it was before the firmament existed (before the spiritual waters were separated from the physical waters).

The same applies to all creations, whether in the spiritual or the physical realms, and even for the inanimate objects of this Earth. If God would remove His creative force, which is constantly giving a created physical or spiritual entity its existence through one of His Ten Utterances, and which keeps it existing at every moment, then that entity would return to nothing.

---

[36] The first part of this chapter is mainly based on *The Gate of Unity and Faith* (*Sha'ar HaYichud Ve'haEmunah*, Tanya, Part II), by Rabbi Shneur Zalman. The second part is mainly based on Maimonides, *Laws of the [Forbidden] Worship of Stars [and Idols]*, ch. 1.

[37] *Ethics of the Fathers* 5:1.

[38] Genesis, ch. 1.

[39] Psalms 119:89.

[40] 1698 – 1760 C.E. He was the founder of the Chassidic movement.

[41] Isaiah 40:8.

[42] From the traditional Jewish liturgy (*Siddur*, in the morning service).

In all respects, the actions of God in His creation of all things are incomparable to those of a human. A human's actions can only change an entity from one created form to another, as in the case of the artisan who takes a block of silver and changes its form into the shape of a vessel. When he finishes shaping the vessel, it leaves his hands, and its existence is not dependent on him, just as the original block of metal was not dependent on him, since he did not create it. God, however, creates the substance and form of the vessel, and the same applies for all of His creations; their existence is contingent on His will to create them *"ex nihilo,"* which is the Latin term for coming into being *"from complete nonexistence"* at every instant. Thus, there is no reason for the created entity to exist other than the power of God's command and utterance which actualizes His will that this entity be created and exist in a particular way. In other words, every particular thing exists through a particular creative force that emanates from God, and that particular force is derived from the much greater general power of His Ten Utterances that are recorded in Genesis, Chapter 1. It is in this way that the Heavenly realms, the universe, our Earth, and all their hosts are created from nothing.

When a person contemplates all the above, he will understand that every individual creation with its particular limitations, as well as the entire limited creation as a whole, both the physical and the spiritual, is accounted as nothing compared to the Godly creative power invested in it. It is that Divine power which creates it *ex nihilo* and gives it existence at every moment, and which is its true reality.

The fact that a created entity appears to us as having a firmly established existence is only because God does not permit us to comprehend or see with our physical eyes the Godly creative force and spirituality that is invested in it to constantly bring it into being. If we would be granted the ability for our eyes to see that Divine energy, even the limited amount which is in an inanimate object, then the entity's physical aspect would not be noticeable to us at all, since its physicality is completely nullified in relation to its source, which is the Godly creative force upon which its existence depends. Without that influence from God, the object would not exist, just as it did not exist before the Six Days of Creation.

Therefore, the Holy One, blessed be He, effects two infinitely powerful actions at once. Everything He creates is brought into existence *ex nihilo* with its individual characteristics, and at the exact same time, He conceals His creative power so that it will not be revealed in the physical realm. Both of these Divine attributes are beyond the comprehension of any created being. For it is impossible for any being to understand the Godly power that gives it existence and life – as God, blessed be He, spoke to Moses, the greatest of prophets, "You cannot see My face, for man shall not see Me and live."[43] And just as it is impossible for any being to understand how it is brought into existence and given life by God's creative power, so too, it is impossible for any being to understand the power of His hiding, with which He conceals the creative force in every creation.

The various Divine attributes which God revealed about Himself are associated with His corresponding Holy Names that are found in the Hebrew scriptures. Any Name ascribed to God is not a description of Him, as it is impossible to describe His blessed Essence, and He has no name which can describe Him at all. Rather, He is ascribed holy Names as indications of various effects that are caused by His actions.

The first Godly power explained above, which constantly creates everything in existence, each in all its details, is called by His holy Tetragrammaton Name of *Y-HVH*. (On account of its great holiness, this Name is not permitted to be pronounced, as explained in *The Divine Code*, Part III, topic 2:7. To refer to this Name orally, and preferably in writing as well, one should transpose the letters into a substitute form, and call it **Hava'yeh**.) The meanings of this Name in Hebrew are that (a) God constantly creates everything that exists, and (b) He transcends time, so that past, present and future are all unified with Him.

The second Godly power mentioned above, the power to hide His unlimited Godly light and creative force – so that we are only able to perceive the effects of His actions in the physical realm, without seeing the true spiritual source which causes and creates these effects – is called by His Name *E'lohim*. This is the source of what we call "nature" within the creation, which is perceivable in our eyes and can be grasped in our understanding, and which hides God's unlimited power and His Presence from us.

---

[43] Exodus 33:20.

This is the meaning of the verse in Psalms, "For a sun and a shield is *Hava'yeh E'lohim.*"[44] This means that just as God made a shield around the Earth that protects us from being obliterated by the heat and radiation from the sun, which are too powerful for us to endure in their full strength, so too, God has a spiritual shield to protect us from the unlimited power of His Divine light and creative force, and this shield is called by the Name *E'lohim*.

Although this spiritual shielding is not physically perceivable, for nature and the world's physicality hide it from our eyes, an intellectual person who contemplates the fact that everything is created by God alone, and that there is no other power to cause any such effect in the world, will understand what is written: "See now, for I, I am He, and there is no [other] God (*E'lohim*) than Me..."[45] Here, God informs us that "I am the Creator, and I am *E'lohim* Who hides My creative power;" He is one and the same God, Who is the only God, with no separation or division. Likewise, it says, "And you shall know this day and take to your heart that *Hava'yeh*, He is *E'lohim* – in the heavens above and upon the earth below – there is nothing else,"[46] so that one should not mistakenly think that there is another power or deity which causes God to be hidden. This is not the case; rather, God Who creates everything *ex nihilo* is also *E'lohim*, Who hides Himself from the perception of mortal beings, through the garb of what we perceive as nature in the physical creation.

This brings us closer to understand the Torah's words, "There is none beside Him,"[47] since His knowledge of the created thing and His Divine speech which creates it are all united as one, within His complete Unity. These two Names, *Hava'yeh* and *E'lohim*, are not separate in any way. Rather, the One God works simultaneously with these two of His powers. Although this concept cannot be fully grasped by human intellect,[48] it is vital for a person to contemplate the principle that God is totally One, such that He and all His seemingly

---

[44] Psalms 84:12.

[45] Deuteronomy 32:39.

[46] Ibid., 4:39.

[47] Deuteronomy 4:35.

[48] Maimonides, *Laws of the Foundations of Torah* 2:10, and *Laws of Repentance* 5:5.

different powers are one perfect entity. The nature of this perfection is something completely unrelated to the creation, because we recognize created entities, and even abstract human concepts, as being composed of different parts that are brought together. This distinguishes God's perfect unity as something completely unique from anything else.

Therefore, a wise intellectual person should unify his whole heart and soul to *Hava'yeh E'lohim*, Who creates the heavens and the earth and all their hosts, and serve Him with all his heart, and dedicate all that he has to serve Him in all aspects of his life. For everything is from Him, and He gives strength, vitality and abilities to each person.

The command given to the Jews, "Hear O Israel: the Lord is our God, the Lord is One,"[49] will in the future reverberate throughout the whole world. The Lord, Who from the time of the Patriarchs has been "our" God (the God of Israel), will in the future be the one Lord over the entire world – as it says: "For then I will turn the peoples to pure language, so that all will call upon the Name of God to serve Him with one purpose;"[50] and it also says, "on that day, the Lord will be One and His Name will be One."[51,52]

From the above explanations, a person should understand the truth and withdraw from misguided and imprudent religious views, such as the views of Enosh and his generation, who thought that the creation was an existence separate from God. From that error, they reached the view that there was a combination of powers in creation along with God, Heaven forbid.[53]

What was the original error of Enosh and his generation? In his days, mankind made a great mistake, and the wise men of that generation gave thoughtless and spiritually erroneous advice. They said that God created the stars and the planets as His means to control the world, and He put them in the expanse of the universe, magnified their greatness, and treated them with honor, making them His servants who minister before Him and administer the world. They reasoned that it is therefore

---

[49] Ibid., 6:4.

[50] Zephaniah 3:9.

[51] Zechariah 14:9.

[52] See Rashi on Deuteronomy 6:4, based on *Sifri*, ibid.

[53] See Rashi on Genesis 4:26.

logically proper for people to praise the celestial bodies, glorify them, and treat them with honor. These people also erroneously decided that it is the will of God that mankind should do this, just as a human king desires that the servants who stand before him should be honored by the common people, for doing so is an expression of honor to the king.

Once this mistaken understanding took root in their hearts, they began to build places to worship the stars and planets, and to offer sacrifices to them. They would praise and glorify them with words and prostrate themselves before them, because by doing so, they would – according to their false conception – be fulfilling the will of God. This was the basis for worship of false gods, and this was the reasoning of those who worshiped them and the explanation that they gave. In those first generations, they would not say that there is no deity other than the star they were worshiping. This is what Jeremiah conveyed: "Who would not fear You, O King of the nations? For [kingship] benefits You; for among all the wise men of the nations and in all their kingdoms, [it is known that] there is none like You. They are uniformly foolish and stupid; the vain [idolatry] for which they are punished, it is [but] wood."[54] This means that all people at that time knew the fact that God exists, but it was from their mistake and their foolishness that they said that this vain pursuit of theirs was God's will.

The mistaken concept of an independent, intermediate power is called a *sheetuf* in Hebrew (literally, a "partner" with God). From this, and their many mistakes and lies which followed from it, they developed the ways and various forms of idol worship. All forms of idolatry are derived and start from this mistaken idea of a *sheetuf*. The general attraction and outcome of belief in a *sheetuf* and the ensuing forms of idol worship was to throw off "the yoke of Heaven" (i.e., obedience to God) from mankind.

In the next (the second) generation, there arose deceitful people – false prophets – who told others that God had commanded them to say: "Serve this particular star or constellation, sacrifice to it, offer libations to it, build a temple for it, and make an image of it, so that everyone – including the women, the children and the common people – can bow down to it." The false prophet would inform them about a visualized form for that star-power (a form that he himself had invented),

---

[54] Jeremiah 10:7-8.

claiming that it had been revealed to him in a prophetic vision. Although the first generation's mistake was "only" the concept that God commanded them to *honor* the stars, the second generation's mistake was the false idea that God commanded mankind to *serve* the stars with such actions as offering sacrifices. This subsequent assertion was clearly a lie, as opposed to the first generation, which only made a mistake with their erroneous thoughts.

In the third generation, other deceivers arose and declared that a specific star, planet, or angel *itself* had spoken to them and commanded them: "The people should serve me in such-and-such a manner." The false prophet would then relate a mode of service he had invented, telling them: "Do this, and do not do this," and these practices spread throughout the world. People would serve their man-made images with strange practices – one more distorted than the other – and offer sacrifices to them and bow down to them. By the fourth generation, God's glorious and awesome holy Name was forgotten by the entire population. It was no longer part of their speech or thought. They no longer knew of God, and they began to serve idolatry exclusively, saying that there is no deity other than the stars, planets, or statues that they worshiped.

It is therefore understood that the first mistake of idolatry is the idea that God wants people to honor a *sheetuf*, and typically this would involve belief in an intermediary that is involved in some way with controlling or influencing the world. But since there are no entities in the higher or lower worlds that have any power without God's authorization and precise judgment, nor any free will to act on their own authority, therefore any power that a physical or spiritual creation may have is only through God's will, which compels it to actively serve its purpose in such and such a way (e.g. the sun to provide light and warmth, and the clouds to provide rain, etc.). Anything that a person may consider to be an intermediary can in truth be no more than an "axe in the hand of the woodchopper" (i.e., a tool in the hand of God), if in fact it has any real effect at all. Therefore, it is not fitting to honor such things at all, since on their own, they are inconsequential in the direction of the world. The only force that is directing the world, from the largest to the smallest scale, is God's will and His power alone, acting through the "tools" He has created.

A false assumption in this area is not only intellectually flawed. It is also intellectual pretentiousness, whereby a person looks for a way to crown himself with the power of a deity – for example, the power to assign other things of his choosing as his deities – instead of accepting obedience to the world's Creator, Who is the one and only True Master over him. Therefore, an upright and intellectually sound person should not believe in any intermediary between him and God, and should not believe that there is some other true existence aside from His, since there is none. Furthermore, if a person has any thought that there is a combination of some other power along with God – even if it is based on a concept that God is the Creator and the Main Power over everything (while some constellation, spirit, chosen human being, or any other secondary power only assists God, but God gave it an ability to act autonomously, even in the minutest way) – this is false and a denial of God's Oneness and Unity. In truth, God is the only True Existence, and there is no other deity with Him.

Worse still are all forms of actual idol worship (among the worst of which is atheism), which causes an even greater separation between the person and God. From this error, or rebellion, is born the attitude that appeals to people in their bad ways, or in the denseness of their perception, that they should not have the yoke of obedience to the True God upon them. Regardless of being raised from birth in an idolatrous religion through no fault of their own, many people are personally attracted to this sin so that they can fulfill the base desires of their hearts without feeling guilt or remorse, and be free from fear of God Almighty. Instead, they willfully accept some other authority or power as their substitute god or gods, and say that their god(s) commanded or permitted the lifestyle which they have chosen for themselves – an alternative to what God commanded for them in His Torah – which may be draped in outward refinement, or set loose to the particular desires that they decide to indulge in.

Chapter 3

DIVINE PROVIDENCE AND TRUST IN GOD

The previous chapter explained the transgression of idol worship and its origin in the mistaken concept of a *sheetuf* (a "partner" with God), through explaining the false concept of independent deities. This concept originates from within a person himself. The influence of a person's evil inclination, and his rebellious thoughts to search for a *sheetuf* of his liking, motivates him not to accept God as the only King over himself, and not to nullify himself to God's will. A person's ego, or "selfness," tells him to be separate in his views and to "be his own boss" – or at least to be somewhat of an "equal partner" with God in judging his actions and deciding which of his desires he will pursue.[55]

In direct contrast to this is the real meaning of the concept of the unity of God within the creation. This is reflected in the unusual wording the Torah uses to describe Abraham's message to the world. The literal translation of the verse is: "And he called in the Name of the Lord, *God universe*."[56] That is to say, Abraham called out that the constant existence of the universe, including the earth we inhabit, is one with the Lord God. If he had used the phrase "God *of* the universe," the people he called out to could have incorrectly taken that to mean that the universe is a separate existence from God, which He governs and watches over. Abraham taught that the universe is not separate from God at all.

The recognition of this truth should be a person's purpose for his entire life, and this should be reflected in all of his actions. One should be constantly focused on and drawn to this outlook of God's unity with the world, with all of one's heart. This is the Divine service that is placed upon every person.

A true recognition of the existence of God in every detail of the world, and in every detail of a person's life, brings a person to a recognition of God's *Divine Providence* over His creations. Simply stated, every entity, with its life and existence, is being constantly created at every moment by God's will and with His knowledge, and it

---

[55] See *Likkutei Amarim* (Tanya, Part I), ch. 24.
[56] Genesis 21:33.

has been previously explained in Chapter 1 that He and His knowledge are One. Conversely, His knowledge of every detail of a thing as it is being created by Him, and of what is happening to it, and His will for it to continue to exist and in a certain condition, are not separate from the thing, but rather are part and parcel of it and cannot be separated from it, in a way that is impossible for us to understand.

These principles are the key to recognizing that God knows and is involved with what is happening in every detail of creation, at every moment, and that everything happens according to His purposeful plan. Not only a person's actions – for example, when someone walks to a certain place at a certain time – but all other events, even the movements of inanimate objects, such as a leaf falling from a tree by the power of a wind and landing in a certain spot, are ordained by God for a specific purpose known to Him. This is the understanding of Divine Providence that was taught by Rabbi Israel Baal Shem Tov.[57]

Through thinking about and looking for Divine Providence in the steps of one's life, a person will recognize that God is actively involved along with him in all his ways, and in all his actions. The majority of the time, a person who does this will understand on his own how to act in the correct and fitting manner for the situation he is in. For when one contemplates that God is watching over him and putting him in a specific set of circumstances at a specific time, and is surely intending for the person to perceive and take action so as to bring out the best outcome from this, it will bring him to try to discern the purpose for which God put him in that situation. For example, it may be to help or inspire another person, or to sanctify God's Name in that place, or to gain the merit of passing a test or overcoming an obstacle which God is placing in his path.[58] When a person sets his mind to this, God in His abundant kindness can give him a spirit of understanding and a feeling for why this situation was intended, and for what he is obligated to do as a servant of God.

Sometimes an understanding of a situation will remain hidden from the person, but if he is righteous and prays to God to enlighten him about its purpose, it is likely that God will show him an answer. In

---

[57] See, for example, *Likkutei Dibburim*, Vol. 1, p. 164, p. 177, in English.

[58] See, for example, the several daily entries on the subject of Divine Providence in the book *HaYom Yom [From Day to Day]*, pub. Kehot.

regard to some things, it may take days, months, or years before God reveals His Divine Providence in something that occurred. Or it may be that God's active involvement in a matter will remain hidden forever, and known only to Him, as King David declared in the Book Psalms, "[Give thanks] to Him Who alone performs great wonders;"[59] i.e., the most wondrous aspect of God's involvement, which may be a chain of actions that span all the previous generations leading up to a present set of circumstances, remains known only to Him alone.

Additionally, when a person contemplates and perceives the continuous Divine Providence which surrounds him, this will bring him to have trust in God. For when he knows that he is not the one in control of his life, but rather it is God, Who created him from the outset and guides him constantly to every place, then he knows that surely the Creator has a purpose for him being in the place and the situation he is in. And if an upright person does not yet understand what the purpose is, nevertheless, he trusts in God that the outcome will be for the best.

A parable for this matter can be drawn from a person traveling in an airplane. If he knows that the pilot is seasoned and trained, he is at peace and trusts and relies on the pilot to bring him safely to his destination. This would not be the case with one who suspected that the airplane had no pilot, and that it was now moving through the air with no control. This person would soon become terrified that any moment the airplane would fall to the ground and he would instantly die. Likewise, a person who is trusting fully in God will be relaxed and serene, since he knows that God is directing him and the rest of the world with infinite wisdom. In contrast, in the parable for one who does not believe and trust in God, as long as his airplane appears to be traveling well, he is at peace. But the moment that it begins to make unsettling movements, he begins to worry greatly about impending doom, and he will lose hope.

The same applies to every individual. A person who thinks that he is the only one who determines his way in life will be peaceful only as long as matters are all in order with the way *he* thinks they should be, since he is putting his trust in his own cleverness or prowess –

---

[59] Psalms 136:4.

although in truth they can't be trusted upon at all. In contrast, a faithful person knows that whether or not things seem to be going well for him at the moment, all matters are directed by God. Therefore he places his trust in God, that He will provide for his every need, and that the end will be for the good and have a good purpose. With this trust, *and in the merit of this trust,* he is peaceful and fully able to pass through every situation of distress and ordeal, whatever it may be.

This is the meaning of what the sages said: "Just as one is obligated to bless [God] for the good, so is he obligated to bless [God] for the bad."[60] Everything comes from God, and everything is for a good end, yet it is to be expected that a person cannot always foresee or comprehend an ultimate good that will come from a trying situation. Regarding the key to internalizing this message, King David said in Psalms: "Many are the pains of an iniquitous person, but one who trusts in God will be surrounded by kindness."[61] A faithful person who experiences pain or troubles will not contest and claim that God is treating him unfairly. For example, he can admit that he has committed iniquities throughout his life, and God in His kindness is now administering some pain that will bring atonement for his unrepented transgressions, so they will not block the greater blessings and rewards that God wishes to bestow upon his soul in the future. This is easy to understand from the analogy of an expert doctor who administers healing that comes only through discomfort, which may be a minor injection or a significant operation. Thus God declares, "I am the Lord your Healer."[62] The much greater depth behind this principle is expanded upon farther on in this book, in the Sixth Gate.

Thus, by way of the contemplation in Divine Providence which brings one to trust in God, one can also control the challenging trait of anger. Anger is the worst trait a person can have, because it causes him to lose his rational thinking and self-control. In his anger, he gives control of himself over to another power – his evil inclination – and he fails to prevent himself from doing what he will sooner or later see was a foolish way to speak or act. In his "heat of the moment," his evil

---

[60] Tractate *Berachot*, ch. 9.

[61] Psalms 32:10.

[62] Exodus 15:26.

inclination shows him a vision of the sweetness that will come from hurting or harming the person who wronged him, but in fact, the primary damage from his anger will come back upon his own head.

Therefore, the sages said: "Anyone who gets angry is as if he served idols,"[63] because during the time of his anger, he abandons his faith and trust in God and sets himself up as the final judge of the situation. This is how his evil inclination is able to become a false god over him, enticing him to bow down to its negative influence. An upright person will keep this in mind and strive to constantly submit his will and actions to be aligned with God's will and wisdom. He grants God dominion over himself, to be a servant of God in all situations.

One should keep prepared in his mind that there can be two negative causes for anger:

(1) A lack of consideration that whatever happens as an actual event in the world is from God's Divine Providence and His will. An angry person is not trusting that God has a higher purpose and intention that can be brought out from the occurrence which he gets angry about.[64]

(2) The person's arrogance, thinking of himself as an independent power, so he becomes angry at anything that encroaches on his influence, honor, authority or opinions.

In summary: anger and pride go hand in hand, and both are the evil outcomes of a person's arrogance, which separates him from God misleads him to place his trust in himself. Humility and tolerance are the traits of a person who trusts and believes in God alone, and knows that everything comes from Him. With this knowledge, he should be able to receive anything from God with forbearance.

Two points should be mentioned to conclude this discussion. First, the path of full faith and trust in God which is described here is the ideal, and in truth it can be an awesome challenge to achieve and maintain. The cause of the greatest challenge in avoiding anger or other loss of trust in God is that every person is biased and not objective about himself, because of his natural inclination to self-love. Therefore, everyone needs a trusted personal advisor, who is a wise and God-fearing person, to whom he can turn for objective advice

---

[63] Tractate *Shabbat* 105b.

[64] See *Igeret Hakodesh* (Tanya, Part IV), p. 276.

about his personal issues and the things that upset him. (In Hebrew, such an advisor is called a *mashpia*.)

Secondly, every trait of a person can be redirected for good, and the correct intention for the emotion of anger is that one should direct it toward his own evil inclination.

Chapter 4

BRINGING RECOGNITION OF GOD INTO ONE'S HEART AND ACTIONS

It is the mandated service of a person to be close to the truth – to be close to God, may He be blessed, the Creator of all, in all his actions and ways. This is the character of upright and righteous people who walk before God: at all times and in any situation, when one is in his house or out pursuing his daily activities, he knows that the Supreme King of kings, the Holy One blessed be He, stands over him and watches all his actions, and searches his heart and his thoughts – as it says: "Can a person hide in secret places so that I will not see him? says God! Do I not fill the heavens and the earth? says God."[65]

A person should contemplate in this fashion during all his endeavors, consciously recognizing that God's watchful eye is stationed over him, and that with this omniscience, God is remembering and judging all his actions. With this mental effort, a person will come to the blessing of fearing God. A person's actions and ways, and his manner of speech when he is with his family and friends, are not the same as when he is in the proximity of a king. How much more so, then, when a person takes to heart that the King of all kings, the Holy One blessed be He, Whose Glory fills the world, stands over him and sees his actions. From his awe of the Creator, he will immediately attain fear and humility before Him, and he will be constantly bashful in His presence.[66]

This is expressed in Psalms 16:8-11, which we explain as follows:

(16:8) "I have placed God before me always; because He is at my right hand, I will not falter." In other words, I have always placed before me the reality that God is standing by me and scrutinizing me. Therefore, I shall not falter or fall into sin or error, and I will not fall into the mistaken idea that I am the one who decides my fate.

(16:9) "Therefore, my heart rejoices, and my soul exults; my flesh, too, rests secure." From this thought, that God is always at my right hand, I am happy and confident, and I have constantly felt serene and self-

---

[65] Jeremiah 23:24.

[66] *Guide to the Perplexed,* vol. 3, ch. 52; *Shulchan Aruch Orach Chayim,* ch. 1.

assured in my heart and soul that I will not err. My body and flesh rests in assuredness, as I know that only good will come from God.

(16:10) "For You will not abandon my soul to the netherworld; neither will You deliver Your pious one to see the pit [of *Gehinom*[67]]." This is Your way, God of truth and kindness, for You will not abandon those who trust in You to cast them away from You; rather You will show them counsel and a way in any situation by which they can rely on You and continue to trust in You.

(16:11) "Make known to me the path of life, that I may be satiated with the joy of Your presence, with the bliss of Your right hand forever." You make known to those who trust in You the way of their service, since they have faith in You and Your Providence which is constantly over them. Therefore they turn to You to ask for counsel and guidance, and You inform them of the correct path in life.

This constant awareness by which a person connects to God does not reside only in his intellectual knowledge. Rather, if it is truly internalized, it will spread to his heart as well, to feel God in his heart – to yearn for Him and to love and fear Him. This is the natural order of how an influence on a person's character progresses. A matter that a person truly thinks to be crucial progressively conquers his inner nature; it begins with constant thought and intellectual contemplation, until it conquers the feelings of his heart, and then his speech and deeds.

It is up to the person's choice that the main concern which influences him should be his desire for closeness to God in all his ways, and not his desire for closeness to the lusts of his evil inclination. Therefore, the sages explained that the Torah's directive to "cleave to God" means that a person should cleave to the holy Torah sages,[68] for he will thereby create an environment for himself that is conducive to influencing his character in the righteous direction we have described. If on the other hand he decides to cleave to people who are hedonistic and immoral, that is the direction to which his character will be drawn.

---

[67] The spiritual Purgatory, where souls receive punishment and cleansing for unrepented deliberate sins which they committed during their life on earth.

[68] See Maimonides, *Sefer HaMitzvot (Book of the Commandments)*, Positive Commandment no. 6.

Likewise, it is said about the knowledge of God, "And you shall know today and take to heart, that the Lord is God, in the heavens above and the earth below, there is no other."[69] The goal of this intellectual comprehension that God enjoins upon us is to fix a love for Him in one's heart, for all of a person's actions are drawn by the heart's emotions. A person will always be quick to do what he loves, and he will withdraw from things that he fears. A person does not experience love for something unless he is yearning for it, and wishful thoughts of it are filling his mind. Likewise, one does not experience fear of a matter unless his thoughts compel him – either out of a fear of danger, or of exposing something he is ashamed of, or from the presence of something of greatness and high honor (i.e., the awe that motivates respect and bashfulness).

A person whose thoughts, feelings and actions are all directed toward one matter is fully focused on it. He is completely "into" it, and in that context, he is identified as person who is "complete" (*shalaim* in Hebrew). But one whose mind is on one matter, while his heart and emotions are dwelling on one or more other things, and his actions are involved in other matters, is therefore disorganized and not complete.

As explained above, a person's completeness (*shalaimut* in Hebrew) can be drawn to the positive or to the negative, according to his choice. A person can place himself into something that is only incidental, or even into something evil, and yet by definition, he is "complete," because he has positioned himself entirely into the mundane thing he is involved in. It is as if he and this natural inclination have combined to become one entity.

An example can be brought of a doctor whose mind is constantly involved with medicine and health; his heart is inspired with emotions to care for his own health and the health of others, and he is constantly reminding himself and others to be involved in healthy matters and to avoid unhealthy things. Regarding such a person, it can be said that he is "Mr. Health," meaning that all his endeavors and constant interest are with bodily health, to the point that if one asked, "Who is this man, and what is he involved with?" he would be answered, "This is Mr. Health." If one would stop this doctor in the middle of his thoughts and

---

[69] Deuteronomy 4:39.

ask what he is currently thinking about, undoubtedly he would answer, "I am thinking about health, and how I'm involved with it."

It is likewise regarding a harmful evildoer, whose thoughts are only evil all day. He meditates on how to damage others by some means, and his heart is filled with wicked emotions. He thinks about how to distress and plague others with great damage in the short or long term, and his actions are directed according to his evil emotions. If people who know this about him were asked who he is, they would respond, "This man is a wicked evildoer."

Consequently, the doctor is completely focused on matters to further health, and the evildoer is completely focused on his wickedness and his effort to do further damage to others. But for both of them, their personal completion is reached through uniting themselves and their faculties with the one thing that they aspire for, and they are involved in it day and night.

By contrast, a person can have thoughts that are partly on one matter, and partly on another, and he has not set his heart to feel one thing in particular. Rather, he has weak emotions about one thing at one time, and about another thing at another time, and there are times when he does not have his full heart in what he is doing. Sometimes his actions follow one thought or feeling, and sometimes another. There are times when there is no connection between his actions and his heart, and he has no prominent feelings that compel him toward the thing he is doing. If one would ask: "Who is this person, and what are his endeavors?" he would surely be answered, "This man is confused, and his character and goals are not known." Such a person is not called complete, but rather mixed-up, because he is only involved with disconnected and superficial thoughts and actions.

A righteous complete person unifies his thoughts and views, to think about God and comprehend His existence, and he will always be aware of God – as King David declared, "I have placed God before me constantly."[70] He should strengthen the direction of his thoughts towards God until he conquers the feelings of his heart, that they should be compelled to follow the direction of his intellect. This unification of his intellect and emotions will bring him to a thirst for God and a yearning to come close to Him. Therefore – from fear of

---

[70] Psalms 16:8.

being separated from God – he will restrict his speech and actions to befit this yearning. In this mode of service, he will be focused all day on God, no matter what mundane activity he needs to be involved with out of necessity at any given time. He will also be looking out for opportunities to do actions that will draw him closer to God, such as deeds of goodness and kindness, and praises of God will be quick to come from his lips in full sincerity.[71] At the same time, he will distance himself, as something that is truly evil in his own eyes, from doing, speaking, or thinking anything that is against God's will or that will be detrimental to his closeness to God. This is the way of a person who is complete in his piety.

When a person becomes upright and complete in this way, and his heart's desire is only to be close to God, his attitudes will align with this. He will acknowledge that this is the ultimate good for him, and he will not be embarrassed or affected by people who ridicule and scoff at him for choosing these pious ways.[72] In spite of them, he will do the things that he knows are consistent with God's truth and God's will, without fear or doubts.

In this way, once the Patriarch Abraham discovered the truth of the One God and connected to it, he was not affected by anything else in the world – as it says, "Abraham was [but] one ..."[73] This means that even though he was distinct from the rest of humanity in his monotheistic faith, and many people, great and small, argued against him and mocked him, he steadfastly continued with the mission he set for himself, since he knew that this path was the truth. This is the ultimate level of one who is completely sincere in his heart and actions, whose sincerity compels him to follow God's will in all matters. Therefore, it is said about Abraham: "And he trusted in God, and He reckoned it to him as righteousness,"[74] and "You found his heart faithful before You."[75]

---

[71] See Rashi on Genesis 39:3 – "[Joseph's] master saw that the Lord was with him," because the name of Heaven [i.e., praise and thanks to God] was frequently in Joseph's mouth.

[72] *Tur Orach Chayim*, ch. 1.

[73] Ezekiel 33:24.

[74] Genesis 15:6.

[75] Nehemiah 9:8.

Once an upright person succeeds in becoming complete in all his actions, and he is continuously yearning for God, he will be truly ready to have self-sacrifice for God. For he understands that anyone's personal pursuits are not the main thing, and that the whole purpose of the existence and importance of mankind is in understanding God to the maximum of one's capability. Therefore, he will devote his whole self to God with all his faculties. He will strongly and constantly desire to rise to God, to the level of Godliness which he cannot comprehend in his intellect and emotions, and before which he stands in a mode of selfless surrender to God.

The ultimate example of this was Abraham the Patriarch, who invested his soul in his mission to publicize the truth that God is One. When he discovered this truth, he started to call to all the populace to leave their idols and vanities and to break their statues. He proved to them with clear and conclusive proofs that their idols were naught and had no power. When Nimrod, the wicked king of Babylon, heard about this, he wanted to silence Abraham, so he seized him and threatened to throw him into a fiery furnace if he would not acknowledge idolatry and bow down to it. Abraham immediately chose the furnace, but a miracle occurred and he was saved. Abraham, however, did not expect this, and he did not have regard for his life if it would mean agreeing to lie and deny the truth for which mankind was created. Abraham reasoned to himself, "What is the point of lying and saving my life, in order to live a life of falsehood? While accepting the falsehood of idolatry, I would be like a broken machine and a soulless walking corpse. If so, my life would be no less than death. It is better for me to die as a means to publicly sanctify God's Name in the world – which has been my lifelong mission – rather than to abandon the truth just to save the physical life of my body."[76]

---

[76] About this, the sages asked how a person could possibly think that he will reach the level of piety of the three Patriarchs. Rather, since everyone does at least have control over his actions, a pious person should instead ask himself, "When will my *deeds* reach the level of the deeds of Abraham, Isaac and Jacob?" (*Tanna D'vei Eliyahu*, ch. 25). That should be the inspiration for an upright person who is striving to be pious before the Lord, his God.

In light of this, one may ask, "Why are Gentiles not obligated to have self-sacrifice for God?"[77]

It is true that God did not *command* this as an *obligation* in the Noahide Code. Nevertheless, if a pious Gentile is complete with the One God in his understanding and emotions, and he has dedicated his actions to be for this end alone, then ultimately, he will not be able to separate from God in a major or minor way, since that would go against his own will and understanding. He knows that he would be ready to surrender his soul to die for God, and he would consider it to be a kindness and an honor, if he would be faced with the choice (God forbid) to either be killed or be forced to submit to a lie of denying God. For everything in comparison to upholding God's truth is self-pleasure and insignificant.

Having the commitment to surrender one's life for God does not apply only to a choice to stand by one's faith in Him or be killed, God forbid. Rather, it is a constant strength of conviction in the consciousness of a pious person, and a firm decision in his heart, not to be separated from the eternal God Who is the True Life of everything. Therefore, a commitment to self-sacrifice is the way a pious person *lives.*[78] He dedicates to God every moment of his life and every breath he takes, looking for opportunities to connect with God and to use his God-given abilities in His service. This is the special greatness in God's eyes of a pious Gentile who is complete with Him in all ways.

---

[77] See *The Divine Code*, Part I (Fundamentals of the Faith), topic 4:3, and Part V (The Prohibition of Murder and Injury), topic 2:9.

[78] It is easy to see how this holds the key to always being able to overcome a temptation to sin. For if a person knows that he is ready to suffer the severe pain of death so as not to deny God, he should be much more ready and able to suffer a much smaller discomfort – namely, giving up a temporary temptation from his evil inclination to transgress against one of the Seven Noahide Commandments. For living by those commandments is a necessity for a Gentile to be able to fully connect on a personal level with God, and conversely, transgressing any of those commandments will separate the person from God (until he repents and makes restitution).

We end this chapter with a quote from the traditional Jewish morning liturgy that precedes the verses of the *Shema* prayer ("Hear, O Israel ..."[79]):

"Our Father, merciful Father Who is compassionate, have mercy on us, and grant our heart understanding to comprehend and to discern, to perceive, to learn and to teach, to observe, to practice and to fulfill all the teachings of Your Torah with love. Enlighten our eyes in Your Torah, cause our hearts to cleave to Your commandments, and unite our hearts to love and fear Your Name, and may we never be put to shame, disgrace or stumbling. Because we trust in Your holy, great and awesome Name, may we rejoice and exult in Your salvation. Lord our God, may Your mercy and Your abounding kindness never, never forsake us."[80]

---

[79] Deuteronomy 6:4.

[80] This Jewish prayer is an expression of the person's constant longing for God. *If a faithful Noahide wishes to say this prayer, we suggest that he should say it with slight changes, according to the following text* (in the Appendix of recommended prayers, see p. 186; this is not the place to explain the reasons for the changes, although they will be quite clear to an understanding person):

"Our Father, merciful Father Who is compassionate, have mercy on us, and grant our heart understanding to comprehend and to discern, to perceive, to learn and to teach, to observe, to practice and to fulfill Your will with love. Enlighten our eyes in Your wisdom, cause our hearts to cleave to Your Seven Commandments, and unite our hearts to love and fear Your Name, and may we never be put to shame, disgrace or stumbling. Because we trust in Your holy, great and awesome Name, may we rejoice and exult in Your salvation. Lord our God, may Your mercy and Your abounding kindness never, never forsake us."

The Second Gate: The Gate of Prophecy from God

Chapter 1

Centrality of Prophecy in the Foundations of Faith; The Concept of Free Choice

It is one of the foundations of faith to know that God gives prophecy to humans.[81] Why is this fact so fundamental?

Prophecy from God, which He bestows upon chosen persons, is His connection to mankind. A person who excels in his service and closeness to God, after cleansing his intellect and heart from the follies and lies of the world, can become a fitting vessel to receive the assistance God wishes to give him to illuminate his path with a higher awareness.

Since God created the world with an intended plan, and it is impossible for a person on his own to know this plan, God's revealing it to mankind is a fundamental imperative. This is the concept of prophecy – a connection of God to mankind by revealing Himself and His ways, through granting knowledge of the Divine.

This correct concept of prophecy also serves to negate the false idea of an intermediary[82] between God and humans. A reason why people originally made the mistake of accepting the idea of an intermediary was that they thought God is too "high" to lower Himself to relate to earthly creatures. From this, they further reasoned that there was no relationship and connection between the Creator and mankind, and no Divine Providence over them. They imagined that God does not truly care about what people do, and that He therefore consigns the governance of the world (totally or partially) to intermediary powers.

The rectification of this error is accomplished when people accept the knowledge which is revealed by God through His true prophets. This brings them to unify themselves with God, and nullify themselves before Him, so they can willfully submit themselves to His purpose

---

[81] Maimonides, *Laws of the Foundations of Torah*, ch. 7. His opinion is that there may be true prophecy among Gentiles as well as Jews; see *Igeret Teiman*: "Therefore, if a Jewish or even a Non-Jewish prophet urges ..."

[82] Explained above in the First Gate, Chapter 2.

and plan. One clear benefit which this brings to a person is the gift of knowing that God's Divine Providence is actively involved with His creations, including each individual person.

God watches over a person, sustaining his life and the direction he chooses, for His desire is that the person will come to choose to live according to His will. Therefore, if a person merits, refining himself to the point that his will follows God's will (which is embodied in the Torah of Moses, as we shall explain), he has unified himself with the Godly purpose and life-force imbued in him – he and these higher dimensions of his existence become one. For such a person, the clarity being revealed to him in his mind and heart is the initial intimation of prophecy. Since he has become a proper vessel to reveal the Godly image within himself, therefore God will open for him true thoughts and correct knowledge.[83]

This is the main concept of prophecy: it is God's bonding of His knowledge with a person's knowledge, and the person's being influenced by this. This is in contrast to the popular conception of prophecy, that it means a prediction of a future event or the performance of a miracle.

The greatest levels of prophecy were attained in the earlier, Biblical generations, by the men and women who were giants of piety. They were able to unite their consciousness entirely to God, Who then imparted a spirit of holiness to them so they could communicate Godliness in human terms to their wider communities. This is the high level of prophecy that is most commonly depicted in the Hebrew Bible (the *Tanach*). It is the most prominent aspect of the *Tanach*, because the concept of authentic prophecy and its characteristics are essential to understanding the truth of the One God and faith in His Torah. Without this, many fundamental themes would be negated, and the unique concept of a religion that is God-given, instead of man-made, would not be correctly understood.

Indeed, Maimonides writes:[84]

---

[83] This is the opinion of Maimonides in *Guide to the Perplexed* regarding the concept of specific Divine Providence over mankind. See *Guide to the Perplexed*, Vol. 2, ch. 17-18.

[84] Maimonides, *Laws of the Foundations of Torah* 7:1.

"Prophecy is only bestowed upon a very wise sage who is strong in his good character traits, whose natural inclinations never overcome him in any worldly matter. Rather, he always overcomes his natural inclinations with his intellect, and he possesses very broad and correct perspective. If a person is completely filled with these good traits and is physically sound, then when he contemplates intently [on Torah's teachings of the greatness of the Creator] and is drawn into these great and sublime concepts, if he has the correct perception to understand and grasp these matters, he will then become sanctified. [That is to say,] he will advance and separate himself from the ways of all the people who go about in the darkness of the times. He must continue to advance and train himself not to have any thoughts at all about empty matters and intrigues of the times. Instead, he keeps his mind constantly directed to a higher level of Godliness in order to comprehend the wisdom of the Holy One, blessed be He ... and appreciate His greatness from this. Then, a spirit of Godly-inspired perception [*ru'ach ha'kodesh* in Hebrew] will immediately rest upon him. When this perception rests on him ... he will be changed into a different person and will understand with a knowledge that is different from what his knowledge was previously. He will rise above the level of wise people in general, as it was told to King Saul:[85] 'You will prophesy with them, and you will be changed into a different person.' "

These words of Maimonides refer to a lofty spiritual level of prophecy and a great prophet, like the prophets of the *Tanach* who prophesied for the Jewish nation and about major issues.

Above and beyond this, the prophecy that ascends above all other prophecies, both in its completion, its message, its quality and the depth of its truth, is the prophecy of Moses our teacher on Mount Sinai when he received the Torah from God, as will be explained in the following chapters. Just as it is one of the foundations of faith to know that God gives prophecy to people at a level that is fitting for each one, according to the refinement of their mind, heart and actions, it is likewise a foundation of faith to believe that it is not only possible that a specific person can reach the highest level of prophecy and conscious connection with God's Presence that is humanly possible, but also that

---

[85] I Samuel 10:6.

God indeed chose Moses as such a person to stand before Him. God gave Moses the ability to spiritually purify himself to the utmost of which a human being is capable, until he reached closeness and constant bonding to God's Presence.

The level of Moses' prophecy made a great unification possible. Through him, God brought His Torah into the physical world. "Torah" is the all-inclusive wisdom of God which includes all the created spiritual and physical realms; it is His Word to all people, forever. It is not directed to a specific person for a specific detail of his activities. It is not even a general concept that affects a person's whole life, being directed to a whole nation or even a whole generation. Rather, it is a prophecy that stands forever as God's will for His creations. It reveals to us that God lovingly created the universe and all aspects of Creation, with this world and mankind at the center of His attention, and with bestowal of obligations, prohibitions, rewards, punishments and purpose. This is the concept of the prophecy that is in the Torah of Moses our teacher, by which God communicated with him openly on Mount Sinai before the eyes and ears of the whole Jewish people, as will be explained in the following chapters.

Aside from the exalted level of the prophecy of Moses our teacher, there are many different levels of prophecy and resting of God's Presence that righteous people could attain. This is analogous to the many different levels of importance of the decisions and concerns that people face in their lives. For example, in this analogy:

– There are times when a person is faced with questions on trivial matters in his daily life, such as what he will eat for breakfast.

– There are times when greater questions arise that involve more important matters in one's life, such as which occupation to choose (e.g., to be a carpenter or a computer technician), and these decisions will have major consequences (e.g., whether he will spend many years training in a school for carpenters, and the condition of his life will be such and such, or if he will be in a different profession, in the company of different people, etc.).

– A person can also be faced with a crucial decision that impacts and changes the whole path of one's life, such as whether to marry a certain spouse, or whether to immigrate to a certain country.

This range of decisions was illustrated in terms of personal concerns of an individual. For a person whose decisions affect the greater community – such as a mayor when he decides to add to a road in the city or construct a building in a certain way – those decisions will impact the residents of the city in many ways. There are likewise many levels of communal decisions, as to how impactful they are and how decisive they will be for the future of the community. At the highest level are national policy decisions made by a head of a country (i.e., a president, prime minister or king) who has the power to give orders that will affect the entire nation, such as whether to go to war against an enemy. The lives of all the nation's citizens, their property and wealth, and their entire future may be dependent on such decisions.

The same concept applies to the resting of *ru'ach ha'kodesh* and prophecy upon a person:

- There can be a question that comes to a person about a personal matter, such as a custom he will follow in his life, e.g., whether to eat breakfast before praying or to pray first and eat afterwards. This is an important spiritual question, and a correct person who is fitting for God to answer him will find the correct answer according to his own level and direction. However, in regard to the person's whole life and his general Divine service, it is safe to say that this is a minor question.

- There can be a great question which will affect a person's whole life and Divine service, such as whom to marry, which will have consequences that will affect one's entire future and conduct.

- There can also be a spiritual question in attaining completion of character, such as how to attain the attribute of humility, or how to distance oneself from the attribute of anger, and he asks for help from God in this matter.

In all these levels of questions, God will put His Providence over an upright pious person and place in his heart and thoughts the advice and help that is befitting him. This is a level of prophecy in the form of God's Presence resting on an individual person.

For larger groups of people there are greater prophecies, of which there are also many levels. There may be a prophecy whose message is for an entire community, but not the entire world, such as the prophecy to the city of Nineveh as related in the Book of Jonah. There can also be a prophecy for the entire world which is for specific matters, having importance in specific ways, such as many of the prophesies in the Books of Isaiah and Ezekiel.

There can also be a prophecy from God for all generations, such as God's directive to Adam the first man on the day he was created, regarding mankind's recognition of Him, and His commanding the first six eternal Divine Laws.[86] These words from God were the revelation of His will in prophecy to Adam, as to what was the purpose of his being created and the mission for mankind in the world.

(From Adam's perspective at the time, this overarching mission was distinct from God's command that he was forbidden to eat from the Tree of Knowledge of Good and Evil in the Garden of Eden,[87] since from the simple meaning of the text, that was a specific command for a limited matter – not to eat from that tree, in that specific place on that specific day.[88] Thus it was presented by God as a small prophecy to a great prophet, since it was only regarding one matter. In contrast, the prophecy in which God first revealed Himself to Adam and commanded upon him six universal commandments, which were given as the directive for mankind's Divine service for all generations, was surely given as a qualitatively greater prophecy. Nevertheless, Adam and Hava's transgression of their prohibition against eating a specific fruit resulted in God's decree of mortality and great difficulties for mankind, for thousands of years until the Messianic Era, may it come speedily in our days. This underscores the advice of the sages,[89] "Be as careful in [observing] a minor commandment as a major one ...")

---

[86] Maimonides, *Laws of Kings* 9:1, quoting from *Genesis Rabbah* 16:6, based on exegesis of Genesis 2:16.

[87] Genesis 2:16.

[88] The sages taught that Adam and Hava (Eve) were only commanded to refrain from eating the fruit of the Tree of Knowledge of Good and Evil until sundown of their first day, which they failed to observe (*Pirush HaShach* on the Torah, *Parshas Kedoshim*; *Or HaChayim* on Genesis 1:29).

[89] *Ethics of the Fathers* 2:1. This refers to the 613 Jewish Commandments, that were from God's speech to Moses (God spoke 10 of them also to all the Jews at Sinai). The 7 Noahide Laws are all major, but the concept applies to Gentiles in regard to directives they receive from God through a true prophet.

Likewise, Noah received prophecy from God that he should be involved with building an ark for 120 years to forewarn the Generation of Flood of the impending consequence of their evil actions, and to save himself and his family from the waters of the Flood. His prophecy was for his whole generation and had great importance for all of them, but nevertheless, it was mainly focused on that period of time within his generation, from the time he started building the ark until the end of the Flood. Surely this was a quantitatively small prophecy in comparison to the greater prophecy to Noah after the Flood, in which God made the everlasting Covenant of the Rainbow – that He would never bring another wholesale destruction of all mankind, leaving only a saving remnant – and He commanded the Seven Noahide Laws. Those were prophecies for all future generations, for the whole world.

It was in regard to greater prophecies, such as those for the needs of a large community, that Maimonides wrote his statement above, that prophecy only dwells on "a very wise sage," etc., who is fitting to receive a prophecy that will guide his generation.

Nevertheless, even a person who does not reach such a level must still know this essential pillar of religion, that God gives prophecy to humans by influencing their thoughts and helping them to choose well and make good resolutions, and He directs them to the greater good if they are improving themselves and humbly striving in that direction. This is the meaning of the verse,[90] "For He stands at the right hand of the needy person to save [him] from those who judge his soul."

Having reviewed the entire range of levels of prophecy that could be granted to a person, we now turn to some major themes that underlie the concept of prophecy.

The first major theme to explain is the true success that is made available for a person to achieve through his freedom of choice. How does this relate to prophecy?

A main point of prophecy is to show that every person intrinsically possesses the ability to serve his Creator in the way that *his Creator*

---

[90] Psalms 109:31. "Those who judge his soul" are a person's good inclination and evil inclination, which pull him toward opposite directions, and God stands by to assist him in following his good inclination, if he so desires.

desires from him, and that by living up to this, he will reach a level of closeness to God, each person according to the capacity that his Creator has endowed to him. One should not think that God has decreed that some people will be wicked or boorish and incapable of properly serving Him. Rather, every person is created as a unique individual to reach his own specific spiritual goals in the face of his own challenges, known to God, and each one is given the ability and the opportunity to complete this service during his lifetime. At the same time, God does not dictate what a person's actions will be. Instead, a person chooses with his own power of choice whether to do good or bad.

From this first essential theme, the power of free choice, one can arrive at a second essential theme: reward and punishment.

God bestows a good reward to those who do good, and He punishes those who do bad; each person is judged by the choices he makes. If everything was decreed by God, and mankind had no free choice at all, there would be no point in reward, since it would not be the person's own choice that brought him to do good. Likewise, there would be no point in punishment, since the bad that was done would not be the fault of the wrongdoer.

These two essential themes will be explained further in the Gate of Repentance, with God's help.

Just as there is reward and punishment in this world or the afterlife for a person's *actions* in this world – that one who chooses to do good deeds and observe what God commands him will merit some type of reward, and conversely, there will be some type of punishment for one who transgresses and does not repent – there is also another type of reward and punishment for the person's spirituality.

God brings close to Himself a good person who acts correctly, and will assist him to do even more good and reach higher levels, and to be successful in his Divine service and to complete the image of God within him. In the opposite case, God hides His face from a bad person and pushes him away, and will make it harder for the person to serve Him, as a punishment for his transgressions. For example, if a pious and righteous person prays to God to show him the correct path in a situation that arises before him, God will answer his prayers and put before him the correct answer, or put in his mind an understanding and feeling for what he should do, or show him in some other manner with Divine Providence.

In contrast, for a bad person who sins many times and defiles himself with evil schemes, if he prays to God when he is in trouble, it is possible that God will answer him out of bountiful mercy, or it is possible that the person's bad ways will cause God to push him away and to put mistakes, doubts and fears in his mind. This is the spiritual punishment for his actions: God will not answer him, or will give him areas in which to make mistakes.

Regarding this concept, God said to Cain: "Surely, if you improve yourself, you will be forgiven, but if you do not improve yourself, sin rests at the door; its desire is toward you, yet you can conquer it."[91] This means that if your path is correct, which is up to your choice, you can receive forgiveness for your sin and correct your failings; but if you do not take a good path, sin crouches at your door, and it is ready and waiting for you to err. So do not say, "This matter is decreed upon me; it is not my fault that I sinned, and I couldn't stop myself from committing the bad action that presented itself to me." Rather, know that your evil inclination only causes you to *desire* to sin, and you can control it and thereby gain merit. The choice of how to *act* is in your hands, not in the hands of your evil inclination.

Likewise, the sages said:[92] "Raish Lakish explained the verse, 'If [one is drawn] to the scoffers, he will scoff, but [if one in drawn] to the humble, he will find favor'[93] – if one comes to defile himself, Heaven will open the way for him, and if one comes to purify himself, Heaven will assist him." This means that if a person looks for a path to defile himself with sin, or to be a scoffer, God will give him the opportunity and open a path for him to sin as he desires, yet this still remains within the person's free choice. But for those who are humble and looking for the right path, God will give them favor and assistance.

God's bestowal of free choice and reward and punishment is understood from the matter addressed in the First Gate, Chapter 3, that there is Divine Providence over all occurrences – meaning that God desires the entire creation and every person individually, including all

---

[91] Genesis 4:7.

[92] Tractate *Yoma* 38b.

[93] Proverbs 3:34.

of one's actions to the minutest detail. Therefore, God unifies His will with the actions of a person, so that when the person performs an action, God's Presence becomes a partner in it. When a person does a good deed, God's desire is apparent in that matter. But when a person does something bad, it is (so to speak) painful to God's Presence that the bad action was done.

Therefore, one should not err like those who think that God left the creation to be directed by the natural order alone, with no Divine Providence guiding it, and that God does not care about people's actions. God's involvement in a person's activities – and even in his thoughts and feelings – provides a spark of prophecy. It can rest on anyone, even those who are considered to be of a lowly level. When a person behaves correctly, God's Presence that dwells in his actions can be perceived, and one who frequently seeks to do good should trust that God will help him and ready a path before him to be successful in his endeavors. However, not everyone merits to be *aware* of this help from God.

When a righteous person prays to God to help him with some matter, God hears his prayer and will help him with his desires for the good. If he merits, he will perceive and understand God's answer and His Divine Providence over him. He should intend to unify with God's Presence through his prayer, as he stands before God and pours out his heart in supplication before Him. He should remove all distracting thoughts, until his thoughts and intentions are pure, and his heart and thoughts are focused in his prayer alone. It was in this manner that the pious ones of the early generations would seclude themselves and concentrate on their prayers to God until they would become removed from physical concerns and achieve a strengthening of their intellectual spirit, until they reached a level of connection to God approaching to the level of prophecy.[94]

---

[94] *Tur Orach Chayim*, ch. 98.

Chapter 2

VARIOUS LEVELS OF PROPHECY[95]

There are many levels among the prophets. Just as there can be one person who is greater than another in wisdom, likewise one person can be greater than another in prophecy. All but the greatest of prophets only receive their prophecy in a vision in a dream at night, or during the day when a great trance falls upon them, as it says, "In a vision I will become known to him, in a dream I will speak to him."[96] When they receive their prophecy, their limbs shake, their body becomes weak, they lose their senses, and their mind becomes clear to understand what it sees. This is what it states concerning Abraham: "and a great, dark dread fell over him."[97] Similarly, the prophet Daniel described his condition when a vision appeared to him: "My appearance was horribly changed, and I retained no strength."[98]

They do not have prophecy whenever they want. If they desire to receive a prophecy, for themselves or someone else, they need to direct their minds to God and sit in seclusion with feelings of happiness. For prophecy does not come to rest on a prophet while he is sad, or lethargic, but rather only when he is happy. Therefore, when the prophet Elisha needed to receive a prophecy, but his mind was agitated, he called for a musician to play for him to settle and uplift his mood. Then he was able to prophesy, as it says, "It happened that as the musician played, the hand of God came upon him."[99]

These characteristics are the ways of all prophets except for Moses, our teacher, the master of all prophets.[100] What was the difference between the prophecy of Moses and that of the other prophets?

---

[95] This is mostly from Maimonides, *Laws of the Foundations of Torah*, ch. 7.

[96] Numbers 12:6.

[97] Genesis 15:12.

[98] Daniel 10:8.

[99] II Kings 3:15.

[100] Possibly, the Messiah, *Mashiach ben David*, will prophesy in manners similar to those described here about Moses, for he will be exceeded only by Moses in his level of prophecy. See Maimonides, *Laws of Repentance* 9:2.

All other prophets experience their prophecy in a dream or a vision, whereas Moses would receive his prophecy while he was awake, lucid and standing – as it says: "Moses came into the Tent of Meeting to speak with Him, and he heard the Voice speaking to Him."[101]

Furthermore, Divine insight *(ru'ach ha'kodesh)* is bestowed through the agency of an angel and is perceived as metaphoric imagery and allegories. But Moses, our teacher, would receive prophecy without the agency of an angel bringing it to him. The Torah testifies to this about him: "God would speak to Moses face to face, as a man would speak with his fellow,"[102] and "Mouth to mouth do I [God] speak to him, in a clear vision and not in riddles; at the image of God does he gaze."[103] In other words, the prophecies to Moses were direct communications to him from God, without being couched in metaphors or allegories, and he would receive God's statements directly and fully. His prophecy would be through direct and open revelation, and he would appreciate the matter in its fullness. Other prophets are overawed, terrified, and confounded by revelations they experience. The response of Moses, our teacher, was not in that manner, but rather, as quoted above, "as a man would speak with his fellow."[104] Just as a person will not be awe-struck from hearing his friend's words, Moses' mental power was so broadly sufficient that he was able to receive and comprehend God's words to him while he was standing in a composed state of mind.

Unlike other prophets, whenever Moses desired, the spirit of *ru'ach ha'kodesh* would envelop him, and prophecy would rest upon him. He did not have to concentrate his attention to prepare himself for prophecy, because his mind was always concentrated, prepared, and ready to appreciate spiritual truth, just as the angels are. Therefore, he could receive a prophecy and relate it to others at all times, as he said to those who needed to hear from him an answer from God: "Stand and I will hear what God will command you."[105]

Moses was called upon by God to be continuously prepared and ready to communicate with Him, as it is stated: "and God said to me, ...

---

[101] Numbers 7:89.

[102] Exodus 33:11.

[103] Numbers 12:8.

[104] Numbers 12:8.

[105] Ibid., 9:8.

'Go say to them, *Return to your tents*. But as for you, stand here with Me, and I shall speak to you ...' "[106] This means that after the Divine revelation of God's speaking the Ten Commandments at Mount Sinai departed from all the rest of the people there (who had been experiencing a state of prophecy while hearing God's voice), they "returned to their tents" like all other prophets – i.e., to their personal bodily needs and mundane activities. Therefore, they did not continue to separate themselves from marital relations with their spouses. Moses, our teacher, however, never returned to his original "tent." He remained in a ready state of holiness to receive God's speech at any moment, so he necessarily had to separate himself permanently from his wife. He bound his mind continuously to God, and the *ru'ach ha'kodesh* was never fully departed from him.

There is the possibility that a prophet will experience prophecy for his own sake alone – e.g., to expand his mental capacities and to increase his knowledge – allowing him to know more about lofty spiritual concepts than he knew before.

It is also possible that a prophet may be sent by God to one of the nations of the world, or to the inhabitants of a particular city or province, to prepare them and to inform them of what they should do, or to warn them against continuing the grave sins which they have been doing. When he is sent on such a mission, God provides a sign or a wonder for him to perform publicly, so that the people will know that God has truly sent him and the message he relates was given by God.

However, not everyone who performs a miracle should be accepted as a prophet, for that is not the criteria that Torah Law sets out. A person who arises and claims to prophesy in the Name of God should be accepted only if it is known beforehand that he is fit to receive true prophecy, i.e., that his wisdom and good deeds are exceptional and consistent with the ways of Torah. If he follows the paths of prophecy in holiness, separating himself from worldly pursuits, and afterwards he states that he was sent with a message from God, and he performs a

---

[106] Deuteronomy 5:25-28.

sign or a wonder, it is a Torah-based obligation to accept that message.[107]

It is also possible that a person who is wise, and who seems to have righteous stature and fitness for prophecy in God's eyes, will perform a sign or wonder even though he is not a prophet sent by God, and the miracle will have another motivation behind it (for example, in answer to his prayers). According to the same obligation from the Torah, we must heed what a person like this is telling us, and accept his statements as true. This can be explained with a parallel concept:[108] Jewish courts are commanded to render a legal judgment based on the testimony of two witnesses. Even though they might be testifying falsely, since we know them to be acceptable as witnesses and they are undisputed in this matter, the Torah Law instructs us to presume that they are telling the truth.

About matters of this nature, it is stated: "The hidden matters are for the Lord, our God, but what is revealed is for us and our children,"[109] and it is stated: "Man sees what is revealed to the eyes, but God sees into the heart."[110]

---

[107] Ibid., 18:15-19.

[108] See Maimonides, *Laws of the Foundations of the Torah* 8:2.

[109] Deuteronomy 29:28.

[110] I Samuel 16:7.

Chapter 3

THE PROPHECY AND TORAH OF MOSES[111]

The everlasting faith that the Jewish people have in Moses, as the preeminent emissary of God,[112] is not because of the miracles that he performed. Whenever a person's faith in a prophet is based on the occurrence of a miracle, that faith is somewhat deficient, because it is possible for someone to bring about a "miraculous" (unexplainable) occurrence through magic or sorcery, or some concealed natural process. This leaves the authenticity of the occurrence as a Divine miracle open to doubt, because there might be some other explanation.

Therefore, the miracles that God performed through Moses, as recorded in the Torah, were not intended to serve as undeniable proof of the legitimacy of his prophecy. Rather, each one was performed to accomplish a purpose that was needed at that point in time. For example, when it was necessary to save the Israelites by drowning the Egyptian army, the sea split for Moses, and after the Israelites passed through on dry land, the Egyptians followed, and God returned the sea upon them.[113] When the Israelites needed water, Moses struck the rock, and it provided a continuously flowing spring of water.[114] When Korach, Dathan and Abiram mutinied against Moses, he called upon God for the earth to open its mouth and swallow them.[115] The same applies to all the other miracles that God performed through Moses.

What then is the foundation of the unique faith in Moses and the Torah he transmitted? It is the public testimony that God Himself gave about Moses during the revelation at Mount Sinai. The entire Jewish people, which numbered over two million adults and all their children, assembled there and witnessed God's Presence and His Divine speech

---

[111] This chapter is based on Maimonides, *Laws of the Foundations of the Torah*, ch. 8.

[112] See Maimonides, *Principles of Faith*, no. 7, and *Laws of the Foundations of the Torah* 7:7.

[113] Exodus 14:15-30.

[114] Ibid., 17:5-6; Numbers 20:9-11.

[115] Numbers 16:28-34.

with their own physical eyes and ears. They all personally experienced that revelation, with each individual verifying the experience of the other. With their own eyes they saw, and with their own ears they heard, as God's voice spoke the Ten Commandments to them, and they heard God saying, "Moses, Moses, go tell them the following ..."[116] Their collective knowledge of God's public appointment of Moses as His emissary was not received as a claim or tradition that Moses or some other individual brought to them. Since they all witnessed it for themselves, that public revelation authenticated the *bona fide* status of Moses as a prophet of God, as well as the Divine origin of the instructions he received from God and recorded in the Torah. Thus it is written: "Face to face did God speak with you [all the Jewish people] on the mountain, from amid the fire. I [Moses] was standing between God and you at that time, to relate the word of God to you, for you were afraid of the fire and you did not ascend the mountain ...;"[117] and "You [the Jewish people] have been shown in order to know ... on earth He showed you His great fire, and you heard His words from the midst of the fire ... You shall [therefore] observe His decrees and His commandments that I [Moses] command you this day ... for all the days."[118]

This foundational principle is alluded to in God's communication to Moses at the burning bush on Mount Sinai, when Moses received his mission from God. At the very outset, God instructed Moses, "This is your sign [to the Israelites] that I have sent you: when you take the people out of Egypt, [that will not be the sign; rather, the sign will be that] you [Moses] will serve God on this mountain."[119] God alluded to him that the miracles of the Exodus from Egypt were intended only as a temporary measure. After they would leave their slavery in Egypt, all the Israelites would stand before Mount Sinai, and their witnessing of Moses being called to serve God upon the mountain would remove any doubts that they had about him up to that point.

---

[116] See Maimonides, *Laws of the Foundations of the Torah* 8:1.

[117] Deuteronomy 5:4-5.

[118] Ibid., 4:35-40.

[119] Exodus 3:12.

Based on all this, the public revelation at Mount Sinai is the only indisputable criterion for believing in and accepting Moses' prophecy and his transmission of God's teachings – as God said to him, "I will come to you in a thick cloud, so that the people will hear when I speak with you and will also believe in you *forever*."[120] Thus, the faith in God's appointment of Moses is undeniable for as long as the Jewish people and their Torah exist, which is forever, and this faith is not based on any miracle that Moses performed. Such a unique testimony to a group of millions of people is impossible to refute, because each overlapping generation serves as the witness to the next generation. Before his death, Moses wrote these events in the first Torah scroll, which God dictated to him, and he made identical copies of that scroll for each of the twelve Jewish Tribes who had personally witnessed and verified the very events which are written there.[121] Thus it is written, "The Torah that Moses commanded us is the heritage of the Congregation of Jacob."[122]

Therefore, if a supposed prophet arises and attempts to dispute or nullify anything in the prophecy or the Torah of Moses (even if he performs great miracles in support of his claim), he should not be believed or heeded. We would know with certainty that his message is false, and that he performed his alleged "miracles" through either magic or sorcery or deception. This conclusion is definite, because the prophecy of Moses was established as true for all time, based on the open revelation of God and His appointment of Moses which occurred publicly at Mount Sinai. In accordance with this, the Torah states about a false prophet: "[Even] if the sign or the wonder comes about, of which he spoke to you, saying, 'Let us follow gods of others that you did not know, and we shall worship them!' – do not hearken to the words of that prophet or that dreamer of a dream, for the Lord your God is testing you ..."[123] The false prophet is coming with signs and wonders to deny what the entire Jewish people know to be true, for their entire population saw it with their own eyes and heard with their

[120] Ibid., 19:9; Maimonides, *Laws of the Foundations of the Torah*, ch. 8.
[121] Deuteronomy 31:9.
[122] Ibid., 33:4.
[123] Ibid., 13:3-4.

own ears, and also verified that it was correctly recorded in the Torah and passed down through all the generations.

But if the message of a supposed prophet is consistent with the Torah of Moses, and he appears to perform a miracle, this person should be accepted as a prophet from that point on based on God's commandment through Moses (as explained at the end of the previous chapter):[124] "A prophet from your midst, from your brethren, like me [Moses], shall the Lord, your God, establish for you – *to him shall you hearken* ... If the prophet will speak in the Name of God and that thing will not occur and not come about – that is the word that God has not spoken; with willfulness has the prophet spoken it, you should not fear him." That is the basis upon which we must accept the message he gives, instead of accepting it based on signs or wonders he performs.

Once the person passes this test,[125] and he fulfills the characteristics of a prophet, we are not to continue testing him every time he gives a new instruction, or when he gives instructions to another group of people in another place. Rather, everyone is obligated to follow the instructions which he gives from then on, as long as he continues to display the characteristics of a prophet, although it isn't known whether the additional wonders he performs (if any) are in fact Divine miracles.

In regard to one who prophesies and it is unknown to the people if he is a true prophet, the same directives in the Torah apply. As explained by Maimonides,[126] "Just as [Jewish courts] are commanded to make a judgment based on testimony of two witnesses, even if it isn't known if they are true or false, similarly, it is a commandment to heed a prophet even though we do not know if the miracle is true or done by magic."

The limitations of what can be a true prophecy, and the types of statements that are sure to be false prophecies, are explained in more detail in the next chapter.

---

[124] Deuteronomy 18:15-22.

[125] The nonoccurrence of a negative event that was prophesied to happen does not disqualify the person who said it in God's Name from being a true prophet. For a negative prophecy may subsequently be annulled through God's mercy, or in response to repentance of the people who have been warned by God of the consequences of their bad ways. This is what happened for the repentant people of city of Nineveh, as told in the Book of Jonah.

[126] *Laws of the Foundations of Torah* 8:2.

Chapter 4

THE ETERNITY OF THE TORAH OF MOSES[127]

It is clear and explicit in the Torah itself (the Five Books of Moses) that it is God's commandment that remains in its original form forever without change, addition, or diminishment – as it is stated, "All these matters which I command to you, you shall be careful to perform. You may not add to it or diminish from it;"[128] and as it is also stated, "What is revealed is for us and our children forever, to carry out all the words of this Torah."[129] This teaches that we are commanded to fulfill all the Torah's directives forever, to the full extent that we are able to do so.

It is also said: "It is an everlasting statute for all your generations,"[130] and, "It is not in the Heavens."[131] This teaches that a prophet can no longer truthfully claim that he has been told by God to add a new permanent precept as being commanded by God.

Therefore, if a person will arise, whether Jew or Gentile, and perform a sign or wonder and say that God sent him to do any of the following, he is a false prophet:

a) add a Divine commandment,

b) withdraw a Divine commandment,

c) explain a Divine commandment in a manner that differs from the tradition received from Moses, or

d) declare that the Divine commandments of the Torah are not forever, but rather were given for a limited time.

A person who calls for any of these things is denying the prophecy of Moses, because he dares to make statements in God's Name that God never made. God, blessed be His Name, commanded Moses that His Torah and its commandments are for us and our children forever, and God is not like man that He will speak falsely.[132]

---

[127] This chapter is mostly from Maimonides, *Laws of the Foundations of Torah*, ch. 9.

[128] Deuteronomy 13:1.

[129] Ibid., 29:28.

[130] Leviticus 23:14.

[131] Deuteronomy 30:12.

[132] See Numbers 23:19.

If so, what is meant by the Torah's statement: "I will establish a prophet for them from among their brethren, like you [Moses], and I will place My words in his mouth; he shall speak to them everything I command him"?[133] A true prophet is not being sent by God to establish a new or different faith, but rather to instruct the people to fulfill their existing commandments in the Torah of Moses, and to warn against transgressing them. Thus, it was declared in the last book of the Prophets: "Remember the Torah of Moses, My servant."[134]

It may be that a prophet will be sent by God to instruct certain people to do something which in that situation is neither commanded nor forbidden by Torah Law, for example: "Go to such and such a place" or "Do not go there;" "Go out to war" or "Do not go out to war;" "Build up a wall" or "Remove this wall." If he has been established as a prophet, it is obligatory to follow his instructions.

Also, if someone who has proven himself to be a prophet instructs us to violate *for a limited amount of time* one or more of the Torah's commandments, whether it be light or severe in nature, it is obligatory to follow his instructions (with one exception, as explained below).

The sages of the early generations taught as part of the Oral Tradition: If a prophet tells you to *only temporarily* violate a precept of the Torah, as Elijah did on Mount Carmel, listen to him with regard to all things except the worship of false gods.

In this example, the *Tanach* relates that Elijah at one time offered a sacrifice on Mount Carmel, which was outside and far away from the Holy Temple, even though the Temple was already permanently designated as the only place for Jews to bring sacrifices.[135] The Torah specifies that a Jew who violates the commandment not to offer a sacrifice outside the Temple courtyard is liable to be "cut off from the midst of his people."[136] But Elijah was already established as a true prophet, so it was obligatory to heed him, since it was clearly a temporary and unique situation. The commandment,[137] "A prophet

---

[133] Deuteronomy 18:18.

[134] Malachi 3:22.

[135] I Kings 18:20-39.

[136] Leviticus 17:8-9. This spiritual punishment to the soul is called *karet* in Hebrew.

[137] Deuteronomy 18:15.

from your midst ... to him shall you hearken," applies in that type of circumstances as well.

If they would have asked Elijah, "The Torah commands, 'Beware for yourself, lest you bring up your burnt-offerings in any place that you see.' How can we violate this?"[138] he would have told them: "The Torah Law is indeed that a Jew who offers a sacrifice outside the Temple premises is liable for his soul to be punished with *karet*. However, the present temporary situation is an exception. I am offering a sacrifice here today by God's instructions, which I received as a prophecy, in order to disprove the false prophets of the idol Ba'al."

If, however, anyone claims to prophesy that a Torah commandment has been nullified forever, he is a false prophet, for the Torah has told us: "[it is] for us and our children forever, to carry out all the words of this Torah."[139] The same applies if someone prophesies that a Torah law which was transmitted as an Oral Tradition from Moses at Mount Sinai is now permanently nullified. In both cases, he is a false prophet and is liable for a capital sin.[140]

---

[138] Ibid., 12:13.

[139] Ibid., 29:28.

[140] The Supreme Sanhedrin was the Jewish High Court of 71 sages, which existed from the time of Moses until it was disbanded due to the Roman oppression after the destruction of the Second Holy Temple. If they convicted a Jew for prophesying falsely in the Name of God, the punishment within Torah Law was execution by strangulation.

The ruling is different for a Gentile, as explained in *The Divine Code*, Part I, topic 2:8 – "Even though a Gentile who prophesied falsely is liable in the judgment of Heaven, the Noahide Code does not include a commandment to judge a false prophet, and ... a Noahide court does not judge [him]. Rather, they are to be judged by a Jewish Supreme Sanhedrin when the required conditions are met. When there is no valid ... Sanhedrin (or if for any other reason they cannot judge the case), if a Gentile prophesies in the name of God to serve idols, or to change one of the Seven Noahide Commandments or to make a new religion, a Noahide court may judge this false proselytizer if the situation requires. If he only prophesies in the name of God falsely, and does not say to add to or change any of the Torah's commandments, but instead speaks about permitted things, it appears to the author that we may only warn him and trouble him to convince him to stop this behavior [and] inform him that he is liable to death by the Hand of Heaven ..."

The same applies if he states with regard to one of the Torah's precepts that *God commanded* him to render a different judgment, or that *God commanded* him about the Torah law regarding a particular issue or that it is to follow a certain opinion. In these cases too, he is a false prophet, even if he performs a wonder, for he is denying that Torah was already given from Heaven by God to the Jewish people at Mount Sinai, and from that point on, "it is not in the Heavens."[141]

If, however, a presumed prophet states that for a limited time we should follow a particular course of behavior, he should be listened to with regard to all things, including all the commandments, except for one. Any prophet who gives instructions or permission to worship any idol should not be heeded, even if he says it is for a limited time. Even if he performs great wonders and miracles when he says that God commanded him or others to worship an idol, be it for only one day or less, it is known that he has "spoken perversely against God."

Concerning this, God commanded in the Torah: "[If] the sign or the wonder comes about, of which he spoke to you, saying, 'Let us follow gods of others that you did not know and we shall worship them,' do not hearken to the words of this prophet ... for he had spoken perversion against the Lord, your God ..."[142] About such a case, the Torah teaches that the so-called prophet is denying the truth of the prophecy of Moses. Therefore, we may definitely conclude that he is a false prophet, and any apparent miracle he did in support of that false instruction was performed by sorcery and magic, or other deceptions.

---

[141] Ibid., 30:12. If a person who does this is a false prophet, how could it be that great Torah sages, including some of those in the Supreme Sanhedrin, were sometimes blessed with revelations of Divine insight in their Torah studies, and even in their opinions that they set forth during debates about questions of Torah law? The answer is that their spiritual insights were put forward for consideration by the other sages, along with the other opinions, and not as Divine commands to be followed without question. Some types of matters within Torah law are commanded to be decided according to the majority opinion among the sages. If a sage put forth a reasoning which he perceived by Divine insight, it was duly considered and debated, and if a majority of the Sanhedrin's members agreed with it, each according to his own rational understanding, it was accepted as the valid majority opinion.

[142] Ibid., 13:3-6.

THE THIRD GATE: THE GATE OF SERVING GOD

Chapter 1

THE ESSENCE OF THE SERVICE OF GOD

It is an obligation for a person to love and fear the glorious and awesome God with all his might.

The inspiration to feel love and fear of God is most effectively achieved by focusing one's knowledge upon Him, while putting his own mundane matters aside. When a person takes the time to contemplate God's wondrous and great deeds, that He is continuously creating and guiding everything that exists in the spiritual and physical realms, and he appreciates that God's eternal wisdom is infinite and surpasses all comparison, he will become inspired to love, praise, and glorify Him. This will bring him to yearn with tremendous desire to recognize God's existence and His attributes, as King David expressed: "My soul thirsts for the Lord, for the living God."[143]

When he then continues his focused contemplation on these matters, he will necessarily recoil in awe and fear through realizing how he is a tiny, lowly and spiritually dark creature, standing with his weak and limited human intellect in the presence of God Almighty, Whose knowledge of everything is perfect[144] – as King David declared:[145] "When I behold Your heavens, the work of Your fingers, ... [I wonder] what is man that You should be mindful of him?"

A person's duty to love and fear the Creator is an intellectual obligation. For when he contemplates that the Creator made the universe for the purpose of establishing the human race, for reasons that came from His Essence, and that the entire creation is nullified before Him and has no separate existence apart from Him, he will recognize that he has been put into existence to be a servant of God. Therefore, a person's greatest advantage and achievement is in fulfilling this mission.

---

[143] Psalms 42:3.

[144] Maimonides, *Laws of the Foundations of Torah*, ch. 2.

[145] Psalms 8:4-5.

However, since it is not in the nature of a person to love or fear something if he does not appreciate its character, it is therefore an obligation for every person to utilize his power of knowledge to contemplate in awe upon the greatness of the Creator, and in humility upon his own lowliness. This is the correct meditation that will bring one to a truthful recognition of God, and this awareness will necessarily arouse feelings that reflect this understanding. In this way, a person draws himself into love and fear of God. As a reward for this service, God will respond and draw the person to Him, and the person will indeed perceive that God's love and awesomeness is being revealed to him from Above, and from within his own mind and heart.[146]

This service to God is not an effortless task. The difficulty to overcome in contemplating the existence of God is that any knowledge that a person attains only comes to him in the context of what he can experience physically, through the senses of sight, sound, smell, taste, and touch. In other words, a person *pictures* in his mind, and *hears* in

---

[146] In the terminology of Chassidic teachings, it is explained that a person's rousing himself from his level below *(isarusa de'latata)* to come closer to God can bring about a much loftier reciprocation from God to rouse the person from Above *(isarusa de'layla),* to give him a greater and higher level of spiritual inspiration for Divine service than he could have achieved on his own. If the person receives this extra inspiration from God and promptly works on himself to internalize it, he can achieve a permanent advance in his spiritual standing. But it is easy for the person to let the gifted inspiration pass with only a temporary effect, leaving him back again at his original level.

It is also possible that God in His mercy and kindness may send a "rousing from Above" to a person who is "stuck in a rut" of habitual sins or bad habits, to fill his heart with a burst of love for God that will give him the strength at that moment to pull himself higher and break out of his lowly ways, so he can become more righteous.

For either way that a "rousing from Above" comes to a person, it is a temporary revelation of God's kind attention. This is not to be confused with the cumulative Heavenly or worldly rewards that are justly given to a person as payment for observing his commandments and doing good deeds over the course of his life.

the thoughts of his understanding, his concept of the matters he learns. Therefore, his knowledge is framed in the context of his own physical existence, surroundings and experiences. As a person contemplates and brings his knowledge of a matter into a more pure and abstract conceptualization and wisdom, his grasp of it will extend, broaden and deepen. But it will never depart totally from being connected to a physical context, because a living person always remains a limited physical being, whereas God cannot be grasped in the context of any human senses.

Therefore, in order to bring the existence of God closer to the grasp of the human mind, it is necessary to employ parables that teach the Godly concepts in terms of human experience. Once the concept of a parable is firmly grasped in a person's understanding, he can apply the point of the parable to a more abstract understanding of the Godly reality. The beginning and most fundamental point is knowledge of God's True Existence, and from this point the heart is able to be awakened to feelings of love and fear of Him.

It was previously explained in Chapter 1 of the First Gate, on Knowledge of God, that a revelation of God in a prophecy needs to be garbed in a physical parable (for example, a vision of God in a human form, or hearing Him speaking in whatever language the prophet knows). This is so that the prophecy will enter the prophet's intellect, from which the point of it can be understood and then communicated in the prophet's own words. A similar intellectual process is even more necessary for a person who is approaching to God on his own initiative. For that can come only from the basis of his own understanding and contemplation of whatever knowledge that he himself has acquired so far.

One of the ways to approach this, which is simple and easily accessible to human perception, is to contemplate God's existence through the analogy of the body and soul of a person. This is the intent of the verse, "From my flesh I perceive God,"[147] which means, "Through contemplating my body and its being kept alive by my soul, which together constitute an 'image of God,' I can gain understanding and perception of the living God Himself."

---

[147] Job 19:26.

A body on its own has no life, for without the soul which gives it life at every moment, it would die. This is not just in reference to the life of the body in general. It also applies to the power bestowed by the individual faculties of the soul, which emanate from its essence and work through the individual bodily functions. The ability of the eye to see, the ability of ear to hear, and all the other faculties of the body (when those organs are in physically correct condition), cannot function unless the power from the corresponding faculties of the soul is resting in and effecting those parts of the body.

The Torah teaches that the creation is like a macrocosm of the body, and without the life-force from God that shines into it, it could not exist for a moment. At its essence, the spirit of life in the universe – which is revealed to us through the functioning of the different powers that are always present in nature – is the creative power of God that gives existence and life to the creation, including everything in the natural world. These powers, such as the constant power in the soil to bring forth vegetation, show that there is a general life-force for the whole world, which maintains the world in existence. The natural powers that we find revealed in the world are extensions of the essential life-force it receives from God, just as the extension of the soul's various powers from its essence serves to give life to the body and animate its numerous individual faculties.

In addition, one can contemplate upon himself and recognize that his body, which is a temporary thing, is secondary and nullified to his soul, since a person's entire life-force, emotions and intellect come from the soul alone. Therefore, by its nature, the body submits itself to follow the directives of the soul (one's will and desires) without opposition, as it is clear that the body has no life of its own without the soul. This contemplation is obvious to a person's perception of the matter, and therefore easy to perform, since a conscious person feels the fact that he is alive, and his life flows constantly from his soul.

One should also contemplate that his body and soul are only details of the general macrocosm which includes the whole world, and that the body's life is a microcosm of the greater life-force for the whole world, which has many levels – inanimate creations, plant life, animal life and human beings, with countless details in each one. This general life-force emanates from God's existence through His creative speech[148] and gives life to every living being and keeps everything in the creation in existence every moment.

Another detail in this contemplation is understood from the analogy that small details in a painting become nullified to the bigger picture in which they are found. A person can recognize that he is but a small detail of the all-inclusive life-force of the whole creation, which in turn is nullified to the existence of the omniscient God. This nullification is infinitely more so than a word of speech from a person, which is nothing in comparison to the entire breadth and depth of his intellect, which is nothing in comparison to the powers of his soul itself. Yet in spite of this, God Himself chooses and cherishes each individual person, and stands over him and watches and analyses each detail of the person's thoughts, words, actions and attitudes, and creates the world for his sake. Therefore, the goal for every person should be to live his life in a way that is correct and good in God's eyes, with the conduct of his body befitting the Godly nature of the general life-force of creation, and God's desire for it.

Why is this? A person is healthy when all parts of his body and their functions are correctly connected and coordinated. Likewise, the spiritual health of the creation is dependent on the coordination of the individual natural powers within it (including the powers of one's own soul), working together as parts of the general life-force that emanates from God's will and desire. A person should conduct his life as being one of God's functions, intended to improve and uplift the people and the society around him, and the creation as a whole. Then, he will not imagine that he is a separate power from God, or removed from the Divine source of life. If that were so, God forbid, the world would be

---

[148] *Ethics of the Fathers* 5:1 teaches: "The universe was created by means of Ten [Divine] Utterances." These are God's statements in Genesis ch. 1 that constantly call everything in the spiritual and physical realms into existence. The ten verses are listed in *Genesis Rabbah* 17:1. The creative life-forces that flow from these everlasting statements are the Hebrew letters of the Divine speech, and the infinite number of combinations that God forms from them. This is explained above (briefly) in the First Gate, Chapter 2, which is based on *The Gate of Unity and Faith* (*Sha'ar HaYichud Ve'haEmunah*, Tanya, Part II), by Rabbi Shneur Zalman.

in a condition like an ailing person; this is the meaning of "From my flesh I perceive God."

(One should not think that giving life to the whole creation is the limit of God's greatness. Rather, He does this only because He desires to reveal Himself to human perception as directing the world with Divine Providence. In truth, His greatness and gloriousness infinitely excel, beyond comparison, His bestowal of life-force and Providence – which itself is far beyond what is revealed and understandable to human beings. Furthermore, the world itself is considered completely naught before Him, as explained in Chapter 1 of the First Gate, in regard to God's "Requisite Existence.")

A person should also contemplate that the totality of everything which God created, with all its details, has a Divine purpose, and what that purpose is. When one understands that God has His own reasons for the creation of the world, and that these reasons are focused specifically on mankind, it will be clear that He has goals which must be possible for people to comprehend and diligently pursue. God, in His love for mankind, gives people the opportunity to choose to serve Him by working for His goals. For that reason, they were communicated by Him to mankind from the outset, as recorded in the Torah of Moses. The goals are also reiterated and supported by the rest of the *Tanach*, which is all words of true prophecy and Divine inspiration.

The sages focused on these messages in their teachings about our universal obligations, such as establishing and spreading kindness and justice in the world, and the like.[149] This contemplation will bring one to the correct recognition of what God desires from him for developing his personal character, his behavior toward other people, and his affect on the world in general, so that he will exemplify the "image of God" in a person.

---

[149] A primary reference is *Ethics of the Fathers*, where we find: in 1:2, "Shimon the Righteous ... used to say, 'The world stands on three things – on Torah, service [of God, which is prayer], and deeds of kindness;' " in 1:12, "Hillel said, 'Be of the disciples of Aaron, loving peace and pursuing peace, loving your fellow creatures, and bringing them near to the Torah;' " and in 1:18, "Rabbi Shimon ben Gamliel said, 'The world endures by virtue of three things – justice, truth, and peace, as it is stated [Zechariah 8:16]: Administer truth and the judgment of peace in your gates.' "

A person needs to express his love to God in his actions and speech that God has gifted to him, for that is their purpose.[150] How should a person accomplish this? The intended Divine service of a person is divided into two categories: that which is directed inward to the person himself, and that which is directed toward God.

The ultimate inward service is the desire, out of love for God, to be close to Him through recognizing and knowing Him. This must be combined with awe and fear of Him, which brings one to the rectification of his natural character and habits, and his deeds in the world. With this combined service of love and fear, a person can reach the high stature of a wise and righteous person.

Service directed toward God is the characteristic of a person who refines himself and is scrupulous to work on revealing his "image of God" with correct actions and correct speech. Such a person is careful not to sully himself like an animal with actions and speech that do not befit an "image of God." With this effort, he rectifies himself and his society, and causes good effects in the world around him. This is how a person contributes to the accomplishment of God's desire for the rectification of mankind and the rectification of the world. One should not imagine that his personal accomplishments in this Divine service are small and insignificant.

Therefore, the truthfulness of one's love toward God is measured by the actions and service it causes him to do. (The service that is specifically done through speech is prayer, which will be explained in the Fourth Gate). The truthfulness of one's fear of God is expressed by refraining from actions and speech that are against His will.[151] By analogy, the truthfulness of one's love for a friend is seen in what he will do and say that is desirable and necessary for his friend, and to what extent he will be concerned about holding back from causing harm or aggravation to his friend.

---

[150] This is expressed in the traditional Jewish liturgy, within the prayer *Nishmat kol chai* ("The soul of every living being"): "Therefore, the limbs which You have arranged within us, the spirit and soul which You have breathed into our nostrils, and the tongue which You have placed in our mouth – they all shall thank, bless, praise and glorify, exalt and adore, hallow and proclaim the sovereignty of Your Name, our King."

[151] *Likkutei Amarim* (Tanya, Part I), ch. 4.

Another subject for contemplation is that lessons can be learned about how people should serve God (and how they should act in their personal lives), from the nature and qualities of various things in creation, including the animals. A primary teaching in this area was given by the sage Rabbi Yehudah ben Tema, who said: "Be bold as a leopard, light as an eagle, swift as a deer, and strong as a lion, to do the will of your Father in Heaven."[152]

What do these things mean?

From the leopard, which uses its boldness for its survival, a person should learn to be bold in the service of God (which is necessary for his spiritual survival), whenever he needs boldness "to do the will of your Father in Heaven." Therefore, one should not be ashamed or bashful when faced with people who scoff at him for serving God and doing the righteous thing. Even though humility is a good trait in general, and brashness in general is a vile trait, nevertheless, for the purpose of doing the right thing in the face of challenges, it is incumbent upon a person to learn from the nature that God put in the leopard. With this he can motivate himself to be bold whenever his natural tendency is to feel embarrassment about other people's denigrating thoughts or comments when they see he is rejecting sin and holding on to moral ways.

From the eagle, which uses its lightness to fly high with ease and swiftness to find and obtain its needs, a person should learn to move easily from place to place, and from one situation to the next, to do virtuous deeds and to be removed from wrong places and situations. One should not be heavy and lazy, and think that once he has already settled or fallen into a certain situation or level, it is acceptable to stay there. Rather, he should learn from the eagle to move on and fly higher in his own ways and in his service to God. A central theme in this is that a person should guard and focus his eyes to only look at good things. Physically, his eyes should dart away and reject sights of immodest and sinful behaviors, both in the outside world and in the world he brings inside through the Internet, movies and television, etc. And in his mind's eye, he should not look for evil in those around him, but rather look for their good qualities from the outset and give people

---

[152] *Ethics of the Fathers* 5:20. From this point to the end of the chapter is based on *Tur Orach Chayim*, ch. 1.

the benefit of the doubt.[153]

From the deer, which is renowned for its swiftness, a person should learn to always be swift and zealous to do good deeds and stay far away from sins. As soon as an opportunity to do a good deed presents itself, a person should swiftly accomplish it and not procrastinate – as the sage Ben Azzai said, "Run to [do even] an easy *mitzvah* (a commandment or good deed), and flee from transgression, for one *mitzvah* brings about another, and one transgression brings about another;"[154] and as the sage Hillel said, "Do not say, 'When I have free time, I will study [Torah],' for you may never have free time."[155] The long-term goal of this contemplation is to habituate oneself to run after good deeds, even pushing oneself to do so, until it becomes second nature.

From the lion, which has great strength and is not afraid of any creature, a person should learn to have strength of heart and not be afraid of any opposition in the world – not those who oppose God's Laws and the ways of justice and goodness, nor one's own evil inclination which does the same – when he truly knows what God desires from him in any situation. So too, Rabbi Eliezer taught his young son, Rabbi Israel Baal Shem Tov, of blessed memory, "My dearest son, ... never fear anyone or anything except the Holy One, blessed be He!"[156]

It is a principle in Torah that "from the positive, one can infer the negative." Just as one can learn good traits from some animals to use in serving God, He put other traits into animals that should be viewed as negative and far below the dignity of any human being. A person can apply those standards as well, in both his private and social ways.

---

[153] In the realm of one's thoughts, and greatly more so in the realm of one's speech, focusing only on the good in another person will actually have the effect of helping the other person to bring out his inner good qualities and to suppress his negative characteristics. And from the positive, one can infer the negative, God forbid. See *In the Garden of the Torah* (pub. Sichos In English), the essay "Inspiring Light" on the Torah portion *Emor* (based on *Likkutei Sichot* v. 27, p. 159ff, and *Sefer HaSichot* 5750, p. 443ff).

[154] *Ethics of the Fathers* 4:2.

[155] Ibid., 2:4.

[156] See *The Light and Fire of the Baal Shem Tov*, p. 19 (pub. Bloomsbury).

Chapter 2

CONTEMPLATION OF THE SEVEN NOAHIDE COMMANDMENTS AND LESSONS FROM THE HEBREW BIBLE

Since a person needs to contemplate the world itself and the natures of its various creatures in order to take lessons from them to improve his service of God (as we explained above), one is even more obligated to contemplate the explicit commandments given to him by God. One must understand from them everything he is obligated to do and forbidden to do, and how to better his character. As Maimonides writes,[157] "Although all of the statutes of the Torah are decrees [from God], ... it is worthwhile to contemplate them, and whenever it is possible to provide a reason, one should provide a reason. ... For most of the Torah's laws are 'exalted counsel' from 'He Who is of great counsel,' to improve one's character and make one's conduct upright."

I will present here some simple contemplations on the Seven Noahide Commandments, and things one can learn from them to rectify his nature and correct his deeds. The reader should not think that these matters are the ultimate intent of the commandments and that there is no more to learn from them, God forbid. Rather, I have written some basic points according to my understanding, based on my studies of these precepts. A wise person should read them and add more lessons for himself.

The primary and most important contemplation is on the very fact that God Himself gave commandments to mankind. This teaches us that God has a purpose for the creation, and He anticipates the time when the world will be brought to its proper rectification. God chose human beings to accomplish this goal through their actions.

Overall, the commandments teach us the lesson that a person is able to do good deeds and rectify himself and his environment. One should not think, in the manner of fools, that a person has no purpose other than to "live for the moment" and cannot accomplish anything of lasting value. Neither should one imagine that people have no free choice and have no effect or purpose at all, like mere puppets of God.

Certainly, a person should not view himself as being inherently evil

---

[157] *Laws of Temurah* 4:13.

from birth, or that it is impossible to improve one's nature. Rather, a person should know and believe that since God commanded him and anticipates his doing specific good actions and refraining from specific bad actions, therefore God surely has given him the power and ability to accomplishing these things in actual fact.

With the following insights, a person can improve his nature and his spirituality as he mindfully observes the Noahide Commandments:

1. The Prohibition of Idol Worship: As explained in *The Divine Code* (Part I, topic 1:5), this commandment includes the command to firmly know and recognize the existence of God. Just as the overall prohibition (including its associated positive command) is first in respect of one's relationship with God, and it is central to accepting the rest of the Noahide Laws as being Divine commandments, one can also derive from it the correct views and advice about all areas of life.

(a) This commandment characterizes a fundamental truth (and by extension this applies for all of the other six commandments), which is that God desires what is truly for the good of a person.

One may ask, "Is there a difference, and does it matter to God, if a person thinks that He exists and that He alone is the True Existence, or if a person imagines it to be otherwise (God forbid)?" But if there is no difference, why is there a need for a commandment in regard to this?!

A person may argue, "If I do not accept God, it is impossible for me to keep any commandments, since I do not believe that there is Divine Authority issuing the commands." That argument is refuted, since it is logically clear that there is only one God Who rules over all, and only He has the unlimited power to bring about everything in His creation. Therefore, in any case, mankind would have to accept God's will and His directives. **Thus the question remains: why did God *explicitly* express His directive to know and recognize His existence, and to negate idol worship, giving it as a *commandment* to mankind?**

God did this in order to give people the gift and the benefit of being *duty-bound*[158] to *Him*, to follow His directive to believe in Him and

---

[158] Being commanded by a higher authority to do something is a totally different level of obligation (and connection with the commander) compared to what a person must do for any other reason. This is explained in regard to Divine commandments *(mitzvot)* in *HaYom Yom*, entry for 8th of *Cheshvan*.

repudiate the idea that there are any other deities.

This teaches us that God's actions can be compared to a loving father who instructs a path of correction and rectification to his child, which he knows is for the good and for the best of the child, for that is what the father desires. By analogy, God gives each person this command, teaching him: "Cleanse your ways from all foreign deities, and unify yourself with the truth that I am the only God. Then you can be with Me constantly, in all your thoughts and actions; in turn, I, God, will be with you if you so desire and are fitting for this."

If God's caring for human beings was not the truth (God forbid), He would merely place His decrees upon a person and force him to comply, like a master who is compelling his slave to submit to his demands against the slave's will, and who doesn't care if the slave is agreeable and happy with complying or not. Instead, in addition to God's wanting a person to take upon himself a general acceptance of His supreme authority and to be a servant before Him, He also wants the person to be complete, rectified, elevated, and refined through being connected to Him – for the person's own good – since He is the ultimate good.

(b) It has already been explained in the First Gate, Chapter 3, what one can learn from the prohibition of serving an intermediary power (a *sheetuf* in Hebrew).

(c) In every action a person takes, he should think about and examine the deed to see how it is further connecting him to God. A person should not think that there is any action which is neutral and does not fall on one side or the other. Rather, when a person is scrupulous and examines his ways, he will see that every action he can take will either be for the good and has a constructive purpose, or (God forbid) is bad and destructive (on some level and in consideration of the outcomes it will lead to).

From this, a person should understand the importance of every action he takes. With this awareness, he should not listen to his evil inclination which tries to persuade him that a particular choice of action is insignificant and makes no difference.

2. The Prohibition of Blasphemy: Logically, this would be an extension of the prohibition of idol worship. Idolatry is separation from God and denial of His sovereignty, and there is no greater denial of His sovereignty than blaspheming God.[159] Why then is this a separate commandment?

The lesson this teaches is the extraordinary power of human speech. Mankind is distinguished from all other worldly creations, not only in his power of intellect and choice, but also in his power of speech.

A person should not think, "The words that I speak are of no consequence." For speech is a special gift that God bestows to mankind, and it should be used only for good, and not for evil. The ultimate ingratitude one can exhibit is using his power of speech to curse the One Who gave him this unique gift. More than that, every person was created in the image of God, and cursing or denigrating another person includes a measure of cursing or denigrating the image of God in that person. This lesson follows from the prohibition of blasphemy – don't curse another person! Since all people are created in God's image, cursing anyone is similar to blasphemy.

This is taught by the following story from the Talmud:[160]

> Once Rabbi Elazar, the son of R. Shimon, was coming from Migdal Gedor, from the house of his teacher. ... He chanced to meet an exceedingly ugly man, who greeted him, "Peace be upon you, my master!" Rabbi Elazar did not return his greeting, but instead said to him, "How ugly this person is! Are all the people of your city as ugly as you?"
>
> "I do not know," he said. "But go to the Craftsman Who made me, and say to Him: How ugly is the vessel which You have made!"
>
> Realizing that he had done wrong, Rabbi Elazar dismounted from his donkey, prostrated himself before the man, and said to him, "You are right. Forgive me!" But the man replied, "I will not forgive you until you go to the Craftsman Who made me and say to Him, 'How ugly is the vessel which You have made.' "
>
> Rabbi Elazar kept on walking after him until he reached his city. The residents of the city came out to greet Rabbi Elazar, saying, "Peace be upon you, O Teacher! O Master!" The man said to them, "Whom are you calling 'Master'?" They answered, "The person walking behind you."

---

[159] As is clear from Maimonides, *Laws of Idol Worship* 2:6.

[160] Tractate *Taanit* 20a (this translation is adapted from www.chabad.org).

He said to them: "If this is a 'Master,' may there not be any more like him in Israel."

"Why?" asked the people.

The man replied, "Such-and-such he has done to me."

"Nevertheless, forgive him," they said, "for he is a man who is greatly learned in the Torah."

"For your sake I will forgive him," said the man, "but only if he does not act this way anymore."

Soon after this Rabbi Elazar entered the study hall and taught: "A person should always be pliant as the reed, and let him never be hard as the cedar."

3. The Prohibition of Murder: This prohibition teaches the value of human life and the honor that is due to every person. This commandment is not limited only to a prohibition of murder. Its branches include not inflicting any bodily harm upon another person. Also, from the positive perspective, one must endeavor to save and help every person from being harmed, to the best of his capability. The obligation that follows from this is the requirement to give proper charity and help those who are needy.

The prohibition of "spilling blood" includes not causing another person's "face to turn red," that is, not to embarrass or belittle someone. Likewise, "evil speech" (*lashon hara*) should not be spoken about other people! This includes gossip, tale bearing and slander, which are considered "assassination of character," and as evil in God's eyes as idol worship, forbidden relations, and murder.[161]

It is taught in the Mishnah:[162] "Adam, the first man, was created alone for the sake of peace among all people; for no one can say to another, 'My father was greater than your father;' ... and [also] to show the greatness of the Holy One, blessed be He, for if a person stamps out many coins from one die, they all resemble each other, but the Supreme King of kings, the Holy One, blessed be He, fashions every man in the image of Adam the first man, and yet not one of them resembles another. Therefore, every person is obliged to say [like Adam, the first man], 'The world was created for my sake.' "

---

[161] Tractate *Arakin* 15b.

[162] Tractate *Sanhedrin* 37a.

4. The Prohibition of Forbidden Relations: The power of pro-creation that God gave to humans is wondrous. With this power, a couple who conceive a child become partners with God in the creation of a new person who will contain the image of God, which is unique and apart from all other types of physical beings. Therefore, humans are somewhat comparable to and partners with God, in joining with Him in the special power to do this. Every precious thing needs guarding and proper respect, and the more precious it is, the more it needs to be guarded from misuse. This teaches the importance of guarding oneself from forbidden relations.

Just as a respectable person would not disgrace himself by running naked and filthy in the streets, so too, a person must not disgrace the abilities that God gives him; instead, he should use his abilities in a way that is befitting and correct as God commanded. This especially applies to intimate relations, which are intended for the bonding of a husband and wife to each other, and through this, for the raising up of children and proper families in society.

If a person does not limit his sexual activities to these goals, he is degrading himself and degrading the Craftsman Who made him, and he sullies his body, emotions and mind, which God created as the vessel for his soul. This is the main area in which we see the foolishness of many people, who destroy their honor and unique human image, because they do not acknowledge the importance of honoring and guarding this wondrous power in the correct fashion. Just as a person can become imprudent from too much wealth or prestige if he does not use those blessings wisely, and it can even make him lose his good senses, the same can happen with a person who becomes animalistic in indulging his lusts, instead of controlling and channeling those desires toward their God-given purpose.

5. The Prohibition of Theft: A person should contemplate that what God has given to another person, he has no need for. Although at times it is hard for a person's mind and heart to agree with this, he should know that this is the truth. He should not desire the possessions and successes of others, but should rather endeavor on his own to reach his Godly ordained potential. From this contemplation a person will come to recognize even more so the Divine Providence over every single person, which has exact design for each person. He should also strengthen himself to constantly trust that God will provide the means for his designated needs.

The following is from *The Divine Code*, Introduction to Part VII:

The prohibition of theft is unique in that it affects almost every aspect of a person's life, since humans ... must deal with each other in buying, selling, exchanging, etc. ... The [main] focus of this commandment is to accept and honor another person, his needs and his possessions. As the Sages taught:[163] "Rabbi Yosay said: 'Let the money of your fellow be as dear to you as your own.' " Theft ... causes corruption that deteriorates and endangers the society ...

... in order to justly accept others as equal to yourself, you must honor them and their property, and this requires inner insight and positive feelings toward others. This comes from recognition that you, exactly like your fellow human beings, are created by the same One God for a general duty and purpose. Therefore no individual is so more important [that he can say] that his needs come totally before the needs of another ... Hence, keeping this command keeps you continuously aware of the Almighty, Who is continuously creating and watching everyone and [guiding] everything with His Divine Providence, for the specific purposes that He expects from mankind in general, and each person in particular.

Another focus of this command [is to] ... contemplate that being just and truthful is not only for the upkeep of society, but also for your own sake and benefit. Being truthful is being correct with yourself, and this makes you fit to recognize your own true virtues, capacities, needs, and duties. ... The only way you can maximize your abilities is by doing your duty in being the person God created for the special purposes He has planned for you, by cleaving to His [Seven] Commandments and the general mode of righteous lifestyle that He assigned for mankind ... But you need a vessel in which to receive this pattern of life, to accept it and manage to live accordingly. This vessel is [your dedication to] truth [and honesty].

6. The Commandment to Establish Laws and Courts: A person should contemplate that God desires just societies, with justice based on standards by which people can agree between themselves as to what

---

[163] *Ethics of the Fathers* 2:12.

is just or unjust. All people are partners in the building of a just society and good behavior. Therefore, this is an obligation upon every person who is capable of influencing others to do good – such as parents who must influence their children – or anyone who has sway over others.

There is another lesson that a person can learn from this commandment. It is possible that a person can ask: "Since God guides everything with His Divine Providence, it must be that the evil that is done in the world surely occurs with His knowledge; if so, why should anyone get involved in the decisions of God?"

In response, this commandment teaches that God wants people to rectify themselves and each other, and therefore He created the world with deficiencies and aspects of evil, so that mankind can serve Him by correcting these things. If a person sees a certain matter which needs to be corrected, he should not say that God, or somebody other than himself, will take care of it. Rather, since it was Divine Providence that God showed him that deficiency, it is clear that its rectification has been assigned to his domain, and that he is fitting to do what is needed, on his own or with the help of others.

7. The Prohibition of Eating Meat that was Separated from a Living Animal: A person should learn from this prohibition not to be cruel to animals, or any other creatures. Even though God gave people dominion over animals, He gave this power to mankind for specific beneficial purposes, and it does not extend to being cruel and causing unnecessary harm or undue pain or distress. (Since this applies to how one treats animals, it therefore applies much more to how one treats other people, regardless of whether it has been placed in his hands to have power and authority over others.)

From the fact that God cares about the pain felt by animals, a person can also learn that He desires a settled establishment of order in the world and rectification of the creatures that He placed within it. Animals are given to mankind to eat and benefit from in other ways, but not to be treated cruelly. By extension, all animals, plants and natural resources have value in God's eyes. It is thus evident that wastefulness is a denigration of God's blessings to mankind, because everything He provides has a special purpose that He intends for it to serve or be used for. Therefore, nothing should be needlessly wasted or destroyed.

The Hebrew Bible: It is appropriate for a pious Noahide to learn the Hebrew Bible (*Tanach*), as it is God's revealed word that He gave to His greatest prophets, and it was written by them with open Divine Inspiration. The Hebrew word ***Tanach*** is the acronym *T-N-Ch*, which stands for *Torah* (referring in this context to the Five Books of Moses), *Nevi'im* (the Prophets), and *Chesuvim* (the Holy Writings). It is full of words of Divine wisdom and lessons for upright behavior, and many of its prophecies are intended for all mankind.

The topics in *Tanach* that Noahides must learn from are not limited to matters of the Noahide Code (as in the examples above). Even those Jewish *mitzvot* that are forbidden for Non-Jews to perform – as well as those that they are permitted to perform voluntarily, but not as commandments from God[164] – can be contemplated in order to learn from them important lessons on how to love, fear and honor God, and how to act righteously toward other people.

For example: Jews are commanded to observe ritual restrictions on their activities during the seventh day of the week (called *Shabbat* in Hebrew). Although Non-Jews are forbidden to take on that ritual observance, there is a great, universal lesson to be learned from it.

The weekly *Shabbat* day teaches us that there is an order and purpose in creation; God created the universe and all aspects of our physical world in six days, and then refrained from continuing this process on the seventh day. Unlike a physical person who gets tired and weary from work, and then needs to take a rest, surely God does not become weary. If so, why did He teach about Himself in the Torah that He "rested"?

In this way, God is showing us that there is an order and a plan in creation, and matters do not happen incidentally, without a purpose. About each of the six days of creation, it is written, "And God saw that it was good." But then God reached the point when He (so to speak) refrained from His "work" of creation, and withdrew from that overall process and contemplated the overall results of His deeds, and He evaluated whether they were good and correct in totality. Of course they were, since God is perfect, but this was to teach an eternal lesson.

---

[164] As explained in *The Divine Code*, Part I, ch. 3, it is forbidden for a Gentile to take anything upon himself as being an observance of a Divine command-ment if it is not included within the Seven Noahide Commandments.

The *Shabbat* was the day on which the assurance was given: "God saw *all* that He had made, and behold it was *very good*."[165]

(Even more so, the tempting of Adam and Hava, and the error that they committed – as well as the consequences that followed from it – occurred before the end of the sixth day. Therefore, with that verse just mentioned, the Torah testifies that this was included in the assessment of *very good* which God bestowed on everything that was made and everything that happened. From this we can see that *all* the actions of God are done with intention and forethought and are not spontaneous, and they accomplish the purpose that God intended. Similarly, it is written,[166] "For as the rain or the snow comes down from heaven and does not return there until it waters the earth, making it bring forth and bud, giving seed to the sower and bread to the eater, so shall be My word that goes forth out of My mouth – it shall not return to me void, but it shall accomplish that which I desire, and succeed in that for which I have sent it.")

Likewise, a person should train himself to always think before acting, with a purpose in mind, and to periodically examine his overall actions to see if their outcomes are good and correct (and if not, how they need to be amended.)

Therefore, the *Shabbat* day is also the source for the concept of repentance. For the first step of repentance occurs when a person takes the time to objectively and truthfully examine the deeds he has done, and the appropriateness and quality of what has resulted from them.

One can also learn from the stories in *Tanach* many lessons in good and correct behavior, as to how one should act, and how one should not act. In particular, the Book of Genesis is also traditionally referred to as *Sefer HaYashar*, the Book of the Upright. When one approaches the reading of *Tanach* with a correct basic understanding (which primarily is provided from the traditional explanations by Rashi), it is correct to say that everything written in all of its books is "exalted counsel from He Who is of great counsel, to improve one's character and make one's conduct upright."[167]

---

[165] Genesis 1:31.

[166] Isaiah 55:10-11.

[167] Maimonides, *Laws of Temurah* 4:13.

Chapter 3

THE VALUE OF ACTION, INTENTION AND HAPPINESS IN SERVING GOD

It is a universal principle that if a good deed is performed without any positive intention involved, it is lacking vitality and is likened to an empty shell. In this vein, the sages taught that "prayer without intention is like a body without a soul."[168] The same applies to all other positive actions; if the person does them without proper intentions, they are considered to be lifeless. What is it that makes this idea so important for the Divine service of Gentiles?

Almost all of the Seven Noahide Laws are negative commandments (things not to do), with the exception of one that is a positive commandment (something to do): Establishing Courts of Justice (*Dinim* in Hebrew).[169] This is in contrast to the Torah Law for Jews, which includes many positive commandments. Even the one positive Noahide Law to establish courts of justice is not a specific physical action, since it is mainly focused on the overall formation of a just society, establishment of just laws, and the prevention of wrong-doing. It is mainly a societal norm, rather than spelling out the actions that are required to fulfill the obligation (although there are offshoots of the commandment of *Dinim* that include actions, such as giving children a good education, etc.). In general, the Noahide Laws do not include the same type of positive commandments as those in which Jews are obligated (for which the obligation itself has specific criteria, such as wearing *tzitzit* fringes, putting on *tefillin*, blowing a *shofar*, etc.)

The Jewish people were sanctified by God at Mount Sinai through being commanded by Him to do these activities (His positive *mitzvot*

---

[168] *Shnei Luchot HaBrit*. For Jews, since they are commanded by God to pray to Him on a daily basis, it is possible that the action of praying is the most important part of the requirement (and even a lack of intention while praying does not constitute a complete deficiency). But for Gentiles, it is clear that the *action* of praying to God is not the main part of the requirement, since there is no specific commandment that a Gentile must perform it. Rather, the main component in God's eyes is the Gentile's intention in his prayer.

[169] See Nachmanides (Ramban), in his explanation of Genesis 34:13, and Maimonides, *Laws of Kings* 9:14.

of the Torah), and He values these *mitzvot* actions greatly when they are performed by Jews, to whom they are commanded. Therefore, when a Jew does them in accordance with their defining details as set out in the Oral Torah, there is intrinsic value to the action itself, since it serves as fulfillment of a Godly command, regardless of the intention involved. (Nevertheless, a lack of intention on the part of the Jew who is doing the *mitzvah* still constitutes a great lack in the *quality* of the action.)

In contrast, a Gentile's deeds are judged by God mostly (indeed, almost completely) in regard to the person's intention, rather than the main focus being upon the specific deed itself.[170] Therefore, in most cases, if a Gentile performs an action without intention, or with an incorrect intention, the action has no positive spiritual value. Since the main obligations of the Noahide Code are logically and morally based, it is by the person's motivating logic and morals that his actions are measured. If his intention is right, the action is judged by God as being good, and otherwise it is not.

(The main and very important exception to this is in giving proper charity and performing acts of kindness for others. This is because the main value in the act is the benefit that accrues to the beneficiary of the charitable giving, and the appreciation of the person who was treated kindly.[171])

For a Gentile, there is no actual holiness in one's action, in and of itself. Rather, the value of the action in God's eyes is based on the intention of the person who does it for a specific purpose, such as for the honor of the Creator, for the benefit of others, for the benefit of his own wellbeing, or for some moral purpose. Nevertheless, every person should accustom himself to habitually do good deeds and act in good ways. Even if good actions are done by rote, or out of habit, they are still considered good actions! This is because the person maintains an overall general intention to do good in his life, even if he doesn't bring a thought about this to the forefront of his mind at the time that he is

---

[170] See Tractates *Rosh HaShanah* 4a and *Bava Batra* 10b.

[171] According to a minority Rabbinical opinion, Gentiles are commanded by God to give charity as a *mitzvah*, in addition to their Seven Noahide Commandments. For a listing of references where this opinion from the Talmud is discussed, see *To Perfect the World*, Part IV, ch. 8 (pub. SIE).

doing the good deed.

The way to avoid slipping into performing actions without proper feelings or intentions is to apply the following practices on a constant basis, or as much as possible: make an effort to be alert to opportunities for doing good deeds; become accustomed to good behavior; and constantly be mindful of your actions and examine them thoroughly, while making sure the intentions behind them are good. By doing so, the person becomes complete in his actions, his emotions, and his ways of thinking. All his faculties thereby become unified in the kind, beneficial actions that he desires to be involved with, as much as possible.

This positive personal completion and unification brings one to a higher level, which is experiencing and maintaining happiness in the service of God.[172]

It is a general principle that when a person experiences happiness, at that time he is personally unified with his situation. (For example: even if he is in the midst of doing something he does not enjoy or care about, and then he suddenly receives very good news, he will temporarily separate from the activity that he doesn't enjoy, and unify his attention with thinking about the good news. Then for as long as he maintains that unity, he will be in a state of happiness.) The opposite is also true. If a person is unhappy, it is clear that his heart and thoughts are not unified with the thing that is occupying his attention.

Thus, even if a person is piously doing good deeds in the service of God, he may be fully dedicated to this but not experiencing happiness. When he realizes and contemplates that what he is involved with is truly for his own good, he will become more *personally* unified with his service, and the proof of this will be seen in his greater happiness.

The same result can be achieved with an alternative approach. When a person accustoms himself to performing good actions and good behaviors with happiness, his happiness has the effect of bringing him to be inwardly unified with his feelings and intentions for serving God. This is the higher nature of a person: the ability to accustom oneself to doing good actions as a matter of habit, until he is complete and unified with them to the point that they become his second nature.

---

[172] This should be one's goal, as it says (Psalms 100:2), "Serve God with joy."

THE FOURTH GATE: THE GATE OF PRAYER

Chapter 1

THE SERVICE OF PRAYER

Prayer is service of God coming from one's soul. Through prayer to God, a person connects his speech, his requests for his needs, and his heartfelt pleas to the Almighty, blessed be He. It is from God that each individual receives his abilities and his accomplishments, and prayer provides the means for a person to strengthen himself in the correctness of his faith and his ways in life.

The main point of prayer is the *service* of the heart. This refers to the *intention* in the thoughts and emotions that motivate the person's prayer. In explaining the verse, "serve Him with all your heart,"[173] the sages said, "What is this 'service of the heart'? This is prayer."[174]

The basic foundation of prayer is that a person needs to explicitly recognize that the One God is the Director of the world and is watching over him, and over everything in the entire creation. Therefore it follows that a person should ask God to grant him all his needs, and thank God for all the kindness and blessings He has bestowed upon him, and also praise Him eloquently, according to his capability.

Unlike Jews, Noahides have no set liturgy (*nusach* in Hebrew) which they are obligated to follow. Rather, each individual can pray in his own words, in a language that he understands. It is proper to include recitation of excerpts from the Book of Psalms by King David, of blessed memory, since the Psalms are all prayers to God that were composed with holy inspiration *(ruach hakodesh)* and encompass all the essential needs and righteous spiritual emotions that people have. Recommended daily prayers were published in *The Divine Code* (Part I, Chapter 6), and more were added in the booklet *Prayers, Blessings, Principles of Faith, and Divine Service for Noahides*. We have included most of these prayers in the Appendix to this book.

---

[173] Deuteronomy 11:13.

[174] Maimonides, *Laws of Prayer* 1:1.

The most appropriate order for prayer is that one should first sincerely praise God according to his capability, then ask for his own needs (and for any blessings that he wishes to request for others), and then conclude with giving praise and thanks for what God has given him.[175]

Due to the importance of prayer, especially when one recognizes its great value – that it is the time for presenting one's self before God, to pour out his supplication and soul to Him – a person should try to the best of his capability to consider himself as standing before the Supreme King of kings at the time of prayer, and to enhance his prayer as much as is possible and fitting in that situation.

One should be attentive to the cleanliness of his body before he begins to pray, which most importantly means that one should not pray while having the urge to relieve himself. Rather, one should first take note and relieve oneself if he needs to do so, then wash his hands, and only then pray afterwards. In fact, every time a person prays, he should first clean his hands by washing them with water (or at least by wiping them with a cloth, if no water is available), whether or not he has relieved himself just beforehand.

One should not pray in an unrespectable place – not in an area of filth, or in a bathhouse, or near a garbage dump, or in an area with a foul smell – and should not be facing such an area when he prays.

It is fitting for a person to establish a set place for praying (even in his own home, to make a private place for prayer), and this area should be respectable. It is even more fitting to pray in an area that has been set aside for the public to pray, if it is nondenominational or consistent with the Torah's principles. (But if a person happens to be in a house of idol worship, it is forbidden to pray there, and one should be careful not to use prayers that were composed by idol worshipers for their liturgies.)

A person should not pray in messy clothes or while he is lacking clothing. If the people in that area would not appear before an eminent person without wearing shoes, he should not pray barefoot. For both men and women, it is not proper to pray with bare arms or legs, as that

---

[175] Ibid., 1:2.

is immodest; instead, one should be clothed respectably, and surely should not pray while naked or nearly so.[176]

It is befitting that every Noahide set time aside for prayer, but there does not have to be any specific time for the prayers. Rather, it is dependent on the current feelings and capability of the person. There are those who feel the need to pray several times a day, during the daytime and at night, and therefore they should. There are others who can suffice with praying once a day. For some, even that is more than they need, and they are not able to have enough concentration if they pray that often, so they find it sufficient to pray once a week.

It is a pious practice (if a person can conform to this) to have a set time dedicated for prayer, once every day. If one is not able to set a time for prayer on a daily basis, then he should set a time for payer on the less frequent schedule which he can observe, such as once or twice a week. The time which is most fitting for this regular prayer is in the morning, at the beginning of one's day.[177]

---

[176] All of the above guidelines apply when a person is praying under normal conditions. But if someone is in a state of emergency, or sick or in pain, or in some other urgent situation, he may pray in conditions for which it is not normally fitting to do so, because the most important aspect of a Noahide's prayer is the intention behind it.

As an example, an exception to the rule of verbalized prayer is if a person is in an area that is designated for people to uncover their bodies or to relieve themselves of their bodily wastes, since those places have an inherent spiritual lowliness. Normally, one should not pray in such places. But if a person is in dire circumstances and has no other choice, and he finds himself forced to pray in such a place, it is better to pray with thoughts only, and not utter the words. For more details, see *The Divine Code*, Part I, topic 6:6.

[177] It is pious practice to set aside some money for charity, in any amount, in conjunction with prayer (see Tractate *Bava Batra* 10a). By doing this before praying, the person will benefit from this extra merit. The Divine service of charity dates back to Abraham, as God said about him (Genesis 18:19): "For I have known him, because he commands his children and his household after him, that they keep the path of God, *to perform charity and justice ...*" Giving properly directed charity (that will not support activities forbidden by Torah) is an act of goodness and kindness, which fulfills the universal obligation to be concerned every day about helping those who are in need, just as we ask God to be merciful to us and fulfill our needs every day.

It is better to pray with a group of people who are coming together for worship to the One God, if that is available (unless one finds that it makes it more difficult for him to concentrate), because their collective merit assists each person's prayers to be more readily acceptable to God.[178]

---

[178] If Noahides establish a local congregation to meet and pray as a group, it is praiseworthy for them to establish a set order of prayers for themselves, with advice about this from Orthodox Rabbis. The staff of Ask Noah International (https://asknoah.org) is available to provide advice and answer questions about prayers and any other matters of Divine service for Noahides. A booklet of congregational services for Noahide communities has been provided, titled *Suggested Prayers for Noahide Community Services and Personal Worship*. As well, the basic order of the selected prayers in the Appendix of this present work can be used for either personal or community services, and in either case, it serves as a recommended starting point if more or different prayers are desired to be included.

Chapter 2

PRAYER WITH SPEECH AND INTENTION

The classical realms of physical existence are the inanimate objects, the vegetation, and the living animals. Torah teaches that the fourth and most important realm in the physical creation is that of mankind, which is referred to as "the speaker" – those who are gifted by God with the power of human speech and human communication. More so, this human ability is a reflection of the realm of Godliness that we refer to as God's "speech," and it reveals the unique connection between mankind and God.

When a person actualizes his power of speech, it serves to unify him, for it is the bridge between the conceptual and the practical dimensions of his existence. This is why spoken prayer connects the deeper parts of one's soul (the inner thoughts and desires) to one's external self, which is involved in the physical action of speaking. It is therefore very important that a person should say his prayers audibly before God, and not suffice with just the thoughts of his heart.[176]

Concentration is needed as a preparation for prayer, in order to be ready to focus one's thoughts on God, the Supreme King. Concentration is also needed as a main part of the prayer itself, together with the verbalization. This means that during prayer, one should focus one's thoughts to the point that they are unified with the words that he is speaking to God. This service of the heart is the essence of prayer, as we quoted in the previous chapter, from the sages of the Talmud: "What is this 'service of the heart'? This is prayer."

The basics of prayer with concentration are twofold: one should position himself in prayer while focusing his mind and staying aware of (a) the One God before Whom he is praying, and (b) what he is praying for. To facilitate this, one should arrange his thoughts before he begins to pray, regarding the things about which he wants to supplicate and pour out his soul before God.

One should not pray while he is in a mood of frivolity, laughter, lightheadedness, hostility, or anger, nor interspersed with scoffing or idle talk. Instead, one should settle down quietly for a little while before prayer and concentrate until he can focus his mind and heart, and only then should he pray. About this, it is related that the early pious ones would tarry for one hour before beginning their prayers,[179] in order to focus their hearts and thoughts, so they could connect all the faculties of their souls with God while praying to Him with humility.

A person should not pray while intoxicated, since one cannot concentrate properly in that condition. Likewise, if one finds that his thoughts are confused due to worries, and he is not able to concentrate, he should delay his prayer until later.

Though it seems that the main point of prayer is for a person to ask for his physical needs, the true main purpose is actually to connect a person with his Creator. One is obligated to ask God for his physical necessities, such as food, livelihood and health, but an even more essential and basic need of every person is his constant connection with God. Therefore one should ask God for this need as well – that God will be with him constantly in all his ways, and that all his ways should be fitting for this. (This is a main theme in the Book of Psalms.)

Prayer is not only a means to ask for and receive this need. One must know that *the prayer itself* is a connection with God.

In conversation and prayer to God, one connects with Him, for God listens to everyone's prayers to Him. He provides for each person's needs in general, and especially this spiritual need for those who feel it and therefore desire that connection. This is the underlying meaning of the sages' statement, "If only a person would pray all day,"[180] because we should constantly have this need in the forefront of our minds. It follows that a person should not let his prayers become a rote chore (i.e., something habitual or coldhearted), but rather a heartfelt supplication before God. About this, the sage Rabbi Eliezer said, "One who makes his prayer into a fixed task – his prayer is not [considered proper] supplication."[181]

Therefore, a main part of prayer is the concentration one should have on the greatness of God and the Truth of His Existence, so that these principles will become set in the person's heart, in all areas of his life.

---

[179] Mishnah *Berachot* 5:1.

[180] Tractate *Berachot* 21a.

[181] Mishnah *Berachot* 4:4.

The Fifth Gate:
The Gate of Personal Traits Desired by God

Chapter 1

The Definitions of Behaving as
a "Wise Person" or a "Pious Person"[182]

Every person possesses many character traits. Each possible character trait is different and distinct from the others, and each one has a corresponding opposite trait. The extremes of these traits can be identified and described.

One type of person is wrathful and constantly angry. In contrast, there is the calm individual who never becomes angry, or, if he does at all, it will be only a slight anger for a very short time, and perhaps that will happen only once in several years.

There is the prideful person, in contrast to one who is exceptionally humble.

There is the person who is ruled by his physical desires, for example, his lusts or his appetite for good food. He is always pursuing his desires without ever being satisfied. Conversely, there is one who is very refined and pure of heart, who doesn't feel a desire for even the minimum sustenance that the body needs.

There is the greedy person, who cannot be satisfied with all the money in the world – as it is stated,[183] "A lover of money never has his fill of money." In contrast, there is the person who puts firm limits on himself to make do with a small amount of money, and he is satisfied with that. Even if it is not enough for his needs, he will not bother himself at all to get more money to obtain what he lacks.

There is the miser, who will torment himself with hunger in order to keep as much wealth in his possession as he can. When he must spend a penny, it causes him great pain. Conversely, there is the spendthrift, who can't spend his money fast enough on wasteful, trivial things.

---

[182] This chapter is based on Maimonides, *Laws of Personal Development (Hilchot De'ot)*, ch. 1.

[183] Ecclesiastes 5:9.

All other traits follow the same pattern of contrasts: for example, elated or depressive, freely charitable or never giving, softhearted or cruel, heroic or cowardly, solemn or flighty, and other traits as well.

Between the extreme of each trait and the extreme of its contrasting trait, there are intermediate points, each distinct from the other. Each individual has a temperament that lies somewhere on the scale from one extreme to the other, and this varies from person to person.

With regard to all the traits, some are inherent in the person's personality from the outset, just as certain physical traits are set from the beginning of his conception to be present in his body. Some are not present initially, but they are a "good fit" to the person's inherent nature and will therefore be acquired more readily than other traits. Some traits will be learned by close association with other people. A person will also come to adopt some traits on his own, as a result of his own ideas. Or he can acquire a trait because he heard from others that it is proper for him to have and that he should strive to attain it, so he practices it until it becomes an integral part of himself.

The two extremes for each pair of traits, which are at a far distance from each other, do not reflect proper paths. It is not fitting for a person to behave in an extreme manner, so he should not push himself into such a direction, nor allow himself to be led there by others. Therefore, if one finds that his nature leans toward one of the extremes or that he adapts easily to it, or if he has learned to act in one of the extreme manners, he should bring himself back to a proper way of acting and go in the path that is followed by good people. This is what is referred to as "the straight path."

The straight path for a person involves analyzing his own traits in all the categories mentioned above, and any others that he has. For each one, he then determines the level of temperament at which he will be equally distant from the two extremes, without being close to either one. That is the middle temperament which he should direct himself to follow. This is the method of self-improvement that was instructed by the early sages, since it is necessary for fulfilling the obligation to be healthy and sound in body and spirit.

For example: one should not be wrathful and easily angered, nor be numb and without feeling. Rather, he should adopt an intermediate target, displaying some limited and fully controlled anger only when a negative matter occurs that is truly serious enough to justify it, for the purpose of preventing the issue from happening again. Similarly, one should only want the physicality that his body truly needs and cannot be healthy without – as it is stated: "A righteous man eats to satisfy his soul, but the stomach of the wicked will feel want."[184]

One should not be overly stingy, nor freely spend his money. He should give charity according to his capacity and lend to the needy as is fitting. He should not be overly elated and laugh excessively, nor be sad and depressed. Rather, he should be quietly happy at all times, with a friendly countenance. The same applies with regard to his other traits.

A person should not become enslaved to his job or career or pursuit of money, always choosing to work overtime, while neglecting his duties in marriage, parenting his children, participating in his community, or preserving his health with enough rest, exercise, and leisure time. One's mind should not be caught up in his business matters day and night. Even if a person's career involves intellectual work instead of manual labor, he should regard it as the external aspect of his efforts, i.e., as if it was a manual type of labor performed with his hands, which he can put down and walk away from when the workday is finished. This is the advice we find in the Book of Psalms, as it says, "If you eat from the work of your *hands*, you are praiseworthy, and it is good for you."[185] (This indicates that work is praiseworthy and good if it is relegated to the external part of the person, represented by the hands, and not consuming one's heart and total priority in his mind.) One's inner focus, contemplation and concern should instead be on Godly matters, including the quality and sufficiency of his prayer, good deeds, and of course his relationship with God.

These ways we have identified as the path on which a person should go, are the ways of those who are wise. Everyone whose traits are intermediate and equally balanced can be called a "wise" person.

A person who carefully examines his behavior and decides to deviate slightly from the middle toward either side, to make an increase in his

---

[184] Proverbs 13:25.
[185] Psalms 128:2.

service to God is called "pious" (a *chassid* in Hebrew). What is implied? One who shuns self-pride and turns more toward the other extreme, and goes about in a sincerely deferential and unassuming way, has achieved a quality of piety. However, if he separates himself from pride only to the extent that he reaches the middle and displays humility, he is called wise, since this is a quality of wisdom. The same applies with regard to other character traits.

The pious people of the early generations would bend their temperaments from the middle path toward either of the two extremes, according to which side is greater in the service of God. For some bad traits (such as anger or haughtiness), they would limit them to the utmost by veering toward the other extreme. For some good traits, they would veer to those extremes (e.g., to be even more humble or charitable than is expected). The sages referred to this manner of behavior with the following expression: "Who is a *chassid*? One who goes 'beyond the measure of the law.' "[186]

The traits that are proper and correct for a person to follow are those by which God is praised in Scripture. The sages said, "Just as the Holy One, blessed be He, is called Merciful, so should you be merciful; just as He is called Gracious, so should you be gracious ..."[187]

In a similar manner, the Biblical prophets called God by other titles: "Slow to anger," "Abundant in kindness," "Righteous," "Just," "Sincere," "Strong," and the like. They did this to inform us that these are good and just paths. A person is obligated to accustom himself to follow these ways and to try to resemble God in these respects, to the extent of his ability.

How can one train himself to follow these temperaments to the extent that they become a permanent part of his personality? He should compel himself to do – and do over and over again – actions which conform to the standards of the middle-range temperaments. He should do this consistently at every opportunity, until those actions are easy for him and do not present any difficulty. When he continues in this way, these temperaments will become integrated into his personality.

---

[186] See Rashi on *Ethics of the Fathers* (Tractate *Avot*) 6:1; Maimonides, Introduction to Tractate *Avot – Shemonah Perakim*, ch. 4.
[187] Tractate *Sotah* 14a.

Since the Creator is called by these terms, and they constitute the straight path which we are obligated to follow, this path is called "the path of God." This is the heritage that Abraham taught his descendants, as God said about him: "For I have known him, because he commands his children and his household after him, that they should keep **the path of God** to perform charity [*tzedakah* in Hebrew, which also means righteousness] and justice ..."[188] One who follows this path brings benefit and blessings from God upon himself, as this verse continues: "... so that God will bring upon Abraham that which He spoke about him," i.e., the promises and the blessings which God gave to Abraham.

"The path of God" is not only the intellectual service of knowing God and His Unity; rather, it includes cleaving to the ways of correct behavior. It is the duty of every person to teach himself and accustom himself to act with correct traits in every area (not just in the examples that were highlighted above). A main goal of this effort is for each person to bring out and reveal the "image of God" in which he is created. Just as a human being cannot live if there is only his head without the organs and limbs that the head depends on, so too with the soul. It is not enough for one's soul to function only as a "head" (in a mode of intellectual Divine service). It also needs to have healthy "organs of the body," which are the correct traits for one's nature and character, and proper "hands and feet," which are the correct deeds that one does – which he should come to do as his second nature.

---

[188] Genesis 18:19.

Chapter 2

HEALING THE SOUL FROM UNHEALTHY TRAITS[189]

To those who are physically sick, the bitter tastes sweet and the sweet tastes bitter. Some sick people even desire and crave things that are not fit to eat, such as earth and charcoal, and hate healthful foods, such as bread and meat – all depending on how serious the sickness is.

Similarly, those who are morally ill desire and love bad traits, and they hate the good path and are lazy to follow it. Depending on how sick they are, they may find it exceedingly burdensome.

Isaiah speaks of such people in a like manner: "Woe to those who call the bad 'good' and the good 'bad,' who take [spiritual] darkness to be light and [spiritual] light to be darkness, who take [morally] bitter to be sweet and [morally] sweet to be bitter."[190] King Solomon described such people as "those who leave the upright paths to walk in the ways of darkness."[191]

What is the remedy for the morally ill? They should go to the wise people, for they are the healers of souls.[192] They will heal them by teaching them how to acquire proper traits, until they return to the good path. Concerning those who recognize their bad traits and do not go to the wise to heal them, Solomon said: "Fools scorned wisdom and correction."[193]

How are they healed? A wrathful person should train himself to feel no reaction even if he is beaten or cursed. He should follow this course of behavior for a long time, until the anger is uprooted from his heart.

---

[189] This chapter is based on Maimonides, *Laws of Personal Development (Hilchot De'ot)*, ch. 2.

[190] Isaiah 5:20.

[191] Proverbs 2:13.

[192] By "wise people ... the healers of souls," Maimonides was referring to the Jewish sages, who have wisdom to help and cure others. It is clear that in practical terms, the teaching cited here applies to any wise person who understands and practices the correct traits for upright people, and the proper ways to correct and cure those who have unhealthy character traits.

[193] Proverbs 1:7.

A person who is full of pride should cause himself to experience much disgrace. He should sit in lowly places, dress in worn-out clothes that shame the wearer, and the like, until the arrogance is uprooted from his heart and he returns to the middle path, which is the proper path. When he returns to this middle path, he should follow it for the rest of his life.

One should take a similar course with any of the other bad traits that he has. A person who swayed in the direction of one of the extremes should move in the direction of the opposite extreme, and accustom himself to that for a long time, until he has returned to the proper path, which is the midpoint for each and every temperament.

Nevertheless, there are a few particular temperaments for which the Torah teaches that a person is forbidden to follow the middle path. He should move away from one extreme and adopt the other. Among these are arrogance and anger (which are the most harmful traits to a person's soul, and they separate a person from God and from other people) – as it says, "God abominates all those who are haughty."[194] Therefore, the sages declared: "Whoever is arrogant is as if he denied God's Presence, as it is stated: 'And your heart will be haughty and you will forget God, your Lord.' "[195]

The early sages[196] said: Anyone who becomes angry is like one who worships idols. They also said: Whenever one becomes angry, if he is a wise man, his wisdom leaves him; if he is a prophet, his prophecy leaves him. And they said as well: The life of the irate is not [true] life.

Therefore, they have directed that one should distance himself from anger and accustom himself not to feel any angry reaction, even to things which naturally provoke anger. This is the good path.

This is the way of the righteous: They accept humiliation, but do not humiliate others; they listen when they are shamed, but they do not answer. They do this with love and accept their sufferings with joy, for this comes from God. About righteous people such as these, it is

---

[194] Proverbs 16:5.

[195] Deuteronomy 8:14.

[196] For a discussion of various sources for these statements, see *Mishneh Torah*, vol. 2 *(Hilchot De'ot)*, commentary by Rabbi Eliyahu Touger, pub. Moznaim.

stated, "And those who love Him are like the sun when it comes out in its strength."[197]

As has been explained above in the Fourth Gate ("The Gate of Prayer to God"), Chapter 2, the power of speech is exceptionally important. Therefore, a person should be very careful with speech, and should cultivate restraint in speaking, except with regard to matters of knowledge or things that are necessary for his physical welfare.

On this point, the sage Rabbi Shimon ben Gamliel said, "I did not find anything better for one's person than silence; ... and whoever engages in excessive talk brings on sin."[198]

Similarly, when speaking about matters of knowledge, one's words should be brief, but rich in content and focused. In contrast, if one's words are many and the content scant, that is foolishness, about which it is stated, "The dream comes with a multitude of subjects, and the voice of the fool with a multitude of words."[199] Likewise, Rabbi Akiva said, "Silence is a safeguard for wisdom."[200]

Therefore, one should not hasten to answer, nor speak at length. If he is a teacher, he should teach his students in calm and tranquility, without shouting or wordiness. This is what Solomon stated: "The words of the wise are heard in tranquility."[201]

A person is forbidden to act in a smooth-tongued and luring manner. He should not speak one thing outwardly and think otherwise in his heart. Rather, his inner self should be like the way he presents himself to the world. What he feels in his heart should be the same as the words on his lips.[202] Therefore, it is forbidden to deceive people. For example, one should not press his colleague to share a meal with him when he knows that his colleague will not accept the invitation, nor should he push presents upon him when he knows that his colleague

---

[197] Judges 5:31.

[198] *Ethics of the Fathers* 1:17.

[199] Ecclesiastes 5:2.

[200] *Ethics of the Fathers* 3:13.

[201] *Ibid.*, 9:17.

[202] This quality of speaking honestly, without hypocrisy, was the praise of Joseph's brothers; see Rashi's explanation on Genesis 37:4.

will not accept them. He should not open honorable drinks supposedly for his colleague, which he is opening anyway for his own purposes, in order to deceive his colleague into thinking that they have been opened in his honor. The same applies with all matters of this sort.

It is forbidden to utter a single word of deception or fraud. Rather, one should have only truthful (yet sensitive) speech, a proper spirit, and a heart that is pure from all deceit and trickery.

One should neither be constantly laughing and a jester, nor sad and depressed. Instead, one should be happy with his lot in life. Our sages declared, "Jesting and frivolity accustom one to lewdness."[203] They also directed that a man should not laugh without control, nor be sad and mournful, but receive everyone in a friendly manner.

Similarly, one should not be greedy, rushing for wealth and possessions, nor lazy and an idler from work. Rather, he should look on things with a good eye, and limit his business endeavors so that he will have time for his spiritual needs and the needs of his family. He should be happy with his lot in life. One should not be quarrelsome, nor envious, full of desires, or pursuing honor. Our sages have said, "Envy, lust and honor-seeking drive a person from the world."[204]

The general principle is that one should follow the midpoint quality of each temperament until all his traits are aligned at the midpoint (with the exceptions identified above, which are anger and pride).

A person might say, "Since envy, lust, the pursuit of honor, and the like, are a wrong path and drive a person from the world, I shall separate from them to a very great degree and move away from them to the opposite extreme." For example, he will not eat meat, nor drink wine, nor live in a pleasant home, nor wear fine clothing, but, rather, wear sackcloth and coarse wool and the like – just as the pagan priests do. This, too, is a bad path, and it is forbidden to go in that way. Whoever follows this path is called a sinner. Therefore, our sages directed that a person should abstain only from those things which the Torah denies him, and should not forbid himself from partaking of permitted things by making vows and oaths of abstinence.

---

[203] *Ethics of the Fathers* 3:13.

[204] Ibid., 4:21.

This general statement also refers to those who act incorrectly by fasting constantly or deliberately causing themselves discomfort.[205] If one feels a need to fast for the purpose of atonement or breaking his haughtiness, it is permissible to do so temporarily, *in moderation,* for he is in the category of those who are ill (as explained above), who need to turn themselves from the middle path to one of the extremes in order to heal themselves, until they have corrected their character.

---

[205] Maimonides, *Laws of Personal Development*, ch. 3.

Chapter 3

GUARDING ONESELF FROM SIN;
GOING BEYOND THE MEASURE OF THE LAW

In the last two chapters, it has been explained that a person should always walk an intermediate path in every trait (with the two exceptions of anger and pride). Nevertheless, the sages instituted various boundaries to distance a person from certain sins.[206] The rationale behind this is that there are some evils from which one needs to distance oneself farther in order not to stumble in them, since most people are drawn by their nature to those types of sins. This follows the principle of the remedy mentioned previously for a person who has an ill trait; his healing can be accomplished by turning from the middle path of that trait, and going to the opposite extreme.[207]

The heart of a man naturally desires forbidden relations, and the sages therefore exhorted people to make boundaries for themselves to distance themselves from this sin. In particular, a man or a woman should not be secluded with someone for whom intimate relations are forbidden to them on account of the commandment prohibiting adultery.[208] The same applies for any case involving a man or woman who has an active desire for a particular type of forbidden relations – someone whom such people would be attracted to for forbidden relations should not be secluded with them.[209] It is true that seclusion without physical contact, with someone for whom physical intimacy is forbidden, is not stated as a Torah-law prohibition for Gentiles. But it is nevertheless wise for one's spiritual health to distance oneself from those seclusions, and to be guarded from any situation that can bring

---

[206] As stated in *Ethics of the Fathers* 1:1, "... make a fence around the Torah." This refers to making extra safeguards in one's behavior so as not to come close to accidentally committing a transgression.

[207] Maimonides, Introduction to Tractate *Avot, Shemonah Perakim*, ch. 4.

[208] See *The Divine Code, 2nd Ed.*, Part VI, ch. 7.

[209] For example, most legal systems prohibit pedophilia, and the courts will prohibit a convicted pedophile from being secluded with a child. This example should be extended as a general practice to those who desire any particular type of forbidden relations.

one to sin. A man is praiseworthy if he is scrupulous and careful not to be secluded with any woman, other than his wife and immediate female relatives. A pious man will follow this even for a woman whom he intends to marry.

Just as there are specific boundaries that were instituted by the sages to distance the general public from certain sins, they also taught that one should observe personal boundaries for himself individually. For example, most people naturally desire to attain monetary wealth, to the point of actively contemplating whether to steal something which belongs to another person. One who feels drawn to this trait should set personal boundaries for himself, so as not to be involved in theft.

Similarly, if one feels a desire to eat flesh from a living animal, he should not even eat the blood of a living animal, or he should eat less meat, in order to lessen the desire. He should continue in this way to train himself to become distant from this lust. This is comparable to someone who is genetically susceptible to alcoholism, and who enjoys alcoholic drinks, who should limit himself so as not to get drunk.

There is another area of life in which it is fitting to go beyond the measure of the law, and not just stay on the middle path, which is in one's interaction with other people. Social interaction is essential, so even if one does not have bad traits in interacting with others, it is proper to behave towards other people in a manner that goes beyond what they deserve. This type of behavior promotes peace in society.

Needless to say, a wise and just person should conduct his business dealings with honesty and good faith. When his intention is "no," he says, "No;" when his intention is "yes," he says, "Yes." But a pious person places additional personal boundaries on his business dealings, beyond the measure of the law. Here are some examples of pious practices:

- He is stringent with himself in his accounting.
- He yields to others when he buys from them, by not demanding his change in full.
- He pays for his purchases immediately, instead of accumulating charges on his bills.
- He accepts obligations in matters of buying and selling, in order to uphold his verbal commitments and not go back on them. For

instance, if he expresses interest to a merchant in buying a product, and then finds the same product from a different merchant at a lower price, he follows pious behavior and still keeps his word to the first merchant, even though that is not required by law.
- If someone has financial obligations to him by law but has difficulty repaying, he grants an extension of the loan, or forgives it completely.
- He lends and bestows gifts, and does so without expecting loans and gifts in return.
- He does not encroach upon another's livelihood, nor does he intentionally cause someone discomfort.
- His general approach is rather to be among the pursued, instead of being among the pursuers, and to be among those who accept humiliation, instead of among those who humiliate.[210]

A pious person who acts this way in business matters, and in other areas as well, causes glorification and honor to his Creator. For these traits of character reflect the ways of God, Who is merciful, gracious, slow to anger, patient and kind – beyond the measure of the law.

---

[210] Maimonides, *Laws of Personal Development* 5:13.

Chapter 4

THE TRAIT OF MODESTY

The trait of modesty is an offshoot of the trait of humility, for a humble person carries himself modestly and does not show off, since that is unbefitting of him. By contrast, a haughty person shows off and is obtrusive in ways that are unbefitting. One who is modest and bashful will honor others, whereas a haughty person who glorifies himself over others and is not modest before them will scoff at them, and is not careful to honor them.

The same applies to a person's deference to God. A modest person is prepared to feel that God constantly watches him and examines his actions and behavior, and therefore he will be bashful and humble before God and will fear Him.[211] Thus it is said, "The result of humility is fear of God."[212] The trait of modesty is obligatory even when one is alone in privacy, and one should always strive to be modest at all times and in all of his ways,[213] because he will thereby train himself to remember the watchful Presence and Providence of God that is over him at every moment.[214]

The trait of modesty must be expressed in all of a person's ways. Primary among these are one's dress, involvements and speech.

---

[211] *Shulchan Aruch HaRav, Orach Chayim* 2:1.

[212] Proverbs 22:4.

[213] *Tur Orach Chayim*, ch. 2.

[214] This is no contradiction to the Mishnaic teaching (from *Ethics of the Fathers* 5:20) cited in the Third Gate, Chapter 1.

This *mishnah* states that one should be "bold as a leopard ... to do the will of your Father in Heaven," yet the same *mishnah* continues and says, "The brazen [person] is headed for *Gehinom*, but the shamefaced [is headed] for Heaven." The two separate concepts are reconciled as follows, as explained in *Likkutei Sichos*, Vol. XV, p. 256: "Humility and boldness need not be contradictory. When it comes to a person's individual concerns, he should be humble and willing to compromise. With regard to his Divine service, however, he should stand proud and boldly assert his rights, remaining unfazed in the face of any and all who try to hinder him." (Translation quoted from *In the Paths of Our Fathers*, ch. 5, pub. Sichos In English.)

How should one be modest in dressing? One should wear clothes that are befitting his rank, and not wear regal garb which draws everyone's attention, nor dress in a manner of poverty which shames the person, nor in a way that is haughty. A person should wear good-looking, middle-range garments.[215]

It goes without saying that a person needs to be modest and cover his body at all times, and not act like an animal that goes unclothed in the street unashamedly. A person has intellect which is his "image of God," and therefore one must dress accordingly, which is to say, honorably. This applies in particular to a woman, so she should cover her body appropriately.[216] When a woman dresses immodestly, she removes from herself the honor of the image of God, and it invites the men who see her to contemplate being involved with her in the sin of promiscuity.

What does it mean to be modest in one's involvements? One should not act in a manner that is ostentatious. Even if a person is very wealthy, he should not display it for the sake of showing off to others. Rather, he should thank God for his success and contemplate in a sensible way about how to use his assets for sustaining himself and his household, and for doing good deeds.

As part of being modest in one's involvements, one must acquire the trait of being satisfied with his lot, and should only desire for himself that which is necessary for the needs of his body and soul. One should not covet the possessions of those who are more wealthy, which are not necessary for him. A person who does so will have a happy and good life, whereas one who desires excesses will not have peace or

---

[215] Maimonides, *Laws of Personal Development* 5:9.

[216] See *The Divine Code, 2nd Edition*, Part VI, ch. 6.

The Torah's standard of modest dressing for women is that the torso would be completely covered with a high neckline, with the arms covered past the elbows, and the legs covered past the knees. These are requirements for Jewish women, but only guidelines (i.e. not strictly required) for Gentile women. Where it is an accepted local custom, a Gentile woman is permitted to wear pants if they at least cover the knees (even when she is sitting down), and they are not immodest. For example, they should not be tight-fitting or otherwise enticing. It is especially pious for a Gentile woman to wear a dress or skirt outfit that is modest above and below.

happiness, because he is always desiring more than he has. The sages have said, "One who has a hundred wants two hundred, and one who has two hundred wants four hundred."[217] The result will be that such a person will never have any satisfaction, because he is constantly chasing after more wealth and possessions than what he has already attained.

Included in this is that one should not chase after honor. The sages warned against this, and declared that "envy, lust and honor-seeking drive a person from the world."[204]

How should one be modest in his speech? One should not shout or shriek like an animal while speaking, nor even raise his voice overly much. Instead, he should speak gently to all people. In addition, he should take care not to stand at a distance when he speaks to someone, lest he appear to be like those who are haughty.

He should greet people before they greet him, so they will be pleased with him. He should judge everyone in a good light and speak favorably of others, never mentioning anything about another person that would cause that person to feel shame. He should follow the directive of the sages to "be of the disciples of Aaron [the High Priest], loving peace and pursuing peace."[218] He should not distort facts, or exaggerate a situation or minimize it, except in the interests of maintaining peace or sparing someone's feelings, or the like.

If he sees that his words will be effective and will be given attention, he should speak; if they will not, he should keep silent.[219] What is implied? He should not try to placate someone who is in the midst of experiencing anger, if it is clear that doing so will cause the person to become even angrier. He should not question someone who is in the midst of making a vow; rather, he should wait until the person's mind is tranquil and calm. He should not comfort someone whose deceased loved one has not been buried yet, because a mourner is emotionally unsettled until after he has buried his dead. He should not look at a

---

[217] Midrash *Kohelet Rabbah* 1:34.

This is a negative trait in regard to a desire for material possessions, but it is a positive trait in regard to spiritual growth and accomplishments.

[218] *Ethics of the Fathers* 1:12.

[219] Maimonides, *Laws of Personal Development* 5:7.

person who is being humiliated, but instead should turn his attention away. The same applies in other similar cases.

In all a person's ways, he should be very modest – as it says, "Walk discreetly before your God."[220] Even literally, regarding a person's manner of walking, he should take care to walk with modesty, and not in a way of haughtiness or attracting attention. One should not walk conceitedly with his nose raised up, nor hunched over. Neither should he run in public like a madman.

From the way a person comports himself, it can be recognized whether he is wise and thoughtful, or mindless and foolish. Thus, Solomon said in his wisdom: "On the road, too, when the fool walks, his mind is empty and he proclaims to all that he is a fool"[221] – i.e., through the emptiness of his personal actions and mannerisms, he informs everyone that he is a fool.[222]

One should act with decency to everyone, and not separate oneself from the acceptable customs and traditions of his community. Likewise, when one travels to another community, he should act in keeping with that community's acceptable customs.

From the above teachings, it is borne out that in every matter, it is to a person's benefit and honor to be modest.

---

[220] Michah 6:8.

[221] Ecclesiastes 10:3.

[222] Maimonides, ibid. 5:8.

Chapter 5

INFLUENCE OF ONE'S ENVIRONMENT; REBUKING ANOTHER PERSON[223]

It is natural for a person's character and actions to be influenced by friends and associates, and to follow the local norms of behavior. Therefore, one should associate with righteous and wise people, and be constantly in their company, in order to learn from their behavior and good deeds. Conversely, one should keep away from bad people who follow bad ways, so as not to learn from their deeds. About this, Solomon said: "One who walks with the wise will become wise, while one who associates with fools will suffer."[224] Similarly, it is stated, "Happy is the man who has not followed the advice of the wicked."[225]

A person who lives in a place where the norms of behavior are bad, and the inhabitants do not follow the straight path, should move to a place where people are righteous and conduct themselves in good ways. If the residents in all the places he is familiar with or hears reports about follow improper paths, or if valid reasons hinder him from moving to a place where the modes of behavior are proper, he should remain secluded from the bad people around him – as it is stated: "Let him sit alone and be silent."[226] Then if it happens that the wicked and sinful people there will not allow him to stay unless he mingles with them and follows their evil behavior, he should "go out to caves, thickets or deserts, [rather than] follow the paths of sinners – as it is stated:[227] 'Who will give me a lodging place for wayfarers, in the desert?' "[228]

---

[223] This chapter is based mainly on Maimonides, *Laws of Personal Development*, ch. 6.

[224] Proverbs 13:20.

[225] Psalms 1:1.

[226] Lamentations 3:28.

[227] Jeremiah 9:1.

[228] This is taken from Maimonides, *Laws of Personal Development* 6:1. Although his advice to live in the wild as a hermit is not practical, it shows the great concern about how much other people can affect someone, and the efforts one must take to distance himself from associating with bad people.

It is important to be associated with righteous people in all of one's involvements, so as to be constantly influenced in a correct and good manner. This includes seeking advice from righteous people regarding one's involvements and path in life.

Just as a person is influenced by his surroundings, so too, every person has influence on others. It is therefore imperative and an obligation for a person to endeavor to have a good effect on the people around him and his society in general, whenever that is possible. One should respect others and guard their honor, and not be cold or indifferent to them, especially when they are in need of positive influence that he can provide. (The converse of this, claiming to be unqualified or unworthy to help when one is really able to do so, is called "false meekness and humility").[229]

It is an obligation for every person not to hate others, and it is surely forbidden to hate without reason (e.g., on account of a person's race). Even if one sees actual wrong in someone's actions or beliefs, he should not hate that person, but instead should endeavor to return the person to the path that is correct according to Torah. If one tries and is rebuffed, he should nevertheless not have any personal hatred toward the person whom he could not return to the right path. Although it is required to distance oneself from a sinner, so as not to be attracted to his bad ways, one should not harbor any hatred toward him, because hatred is also an evil trait that comes from the evil inclination; it leads to disputes, fighting, bigotry, and many other bad things.[230]

(One is, however, obligated to differentiate between people who sin between themselves and God, and do little or no harm to others, versus extremely evil people who cause harm to society and cannot be

---

[229] This expression is used in this context in the Compiler's Forward to *Likkutei Amarim* (Tanya, Part I); see *Chovos Halevavos*, Introduction to the "Gate of Humility."

[230] See *Likkutei Amarim* (Tanya, Part I), ch. 32, regarding the commandment for a Jew to always love his fellow Jew. In that case, if hatred is obligatory on account of an individual's stubbornness to continue sinning even after repeated rebuke from his colleague, the love for him must continue to be maintained as well. Although Gentiles are not commanded to love each other, this serves as a lesson for pious behavior amongst them as well.

corrected through any conventional means, such as bringing them to justice or a justified rebuke from the community and its leaders. Those types of evildoers should be hated by as many people as possible, in order that everyone will learn to stay distant from them and from their evil actions.)[231]

When one person wrongs another, the latter should not remain silent. Rather, he should bring it to the attention of the offender and ask him: "Why did you do this to me? Why did you wrong me regarding that matter?" If, afterwards, the person who was at fault asks to be forgiven, he should be forgiven. A person should not harbor ill will and not forgive, as is implied by the verse, "And Abraham prayed to God ..."[232] (to heal Abimelech who had unwittingly wronged him).

As explained in *The Divine Code*,[233] it is an obligation to rebuke a person for sinning in matters that are forbidden by the Noahide Code, if that could convince him to stop. This follows from the Noahide commandment for Gentiles to establish a just and correct society. Whoever has the opportunity to successfully rebuke a sinner but refrains from doing so, is considered responsible for a sin which he could have prevented, if he would have given the rebuke.[234]

Therefore, it is righteous behavior for a person who sees that his fellow has sinned, or is following an improper path, to attempt to correct his behavior and to inform him that he is causing himself a loss by his bad deeds – as it is stated: "You shall surely admonish your fellow ..."[235] This applies whether the sinner is of the same, greater, or lesser stature than the person who gives the rebuke. However, one is only obligated to admonish a person with whom he is acquainted. If the wrongdoer is a stranger who will hate him for giving the admonishment, and who may take revenge on him, then one need not admonish this person unless it will surely be accepted.[236]

A person who rebukes a colleague – whether because of a wrong

---

[231] See *Likkutei Amarim* (Tanya, Part I), end of ch. 32.

[232] Genesis 20:17.

[233] Part I, topics 3:1 and 4:8.

[234] See Maimonides, *Laws of Kings* 9:14, in regard to the people of Shechem.

[235] Leviticus 19:17.

[236] *Shulchan Aruch HaRav, Orach Chayim* 156:7.

committed against him, or against another person, or because of a matter between his colleague and God – should rebuke him privately. He should speak to him patiently and gently, informing him that he is only making these statements for his colleague's own welfare, to help him merit the life of the World to Come. If he accepts the rebuke, it is good; if not, he should rebuke him a second and third time. Indeed, one is obligated to rebuke a colleague who does wrong until the latter strikes him and tells him, "I will not listen!" or a similar statement that implies that he will no longer tolerate being rebuked. When one sees that the sinner is not accepting the rebuke at all, there is no obligation to continue or try harder.

A person who admonishes a colleague should not speak to him harshly until he becomes embarrassed, as the above-cited verse states (in full), "You shall surely admonish your fellow, and [do] not bear a sin because of him;" i.e., do not admonish him in a way that will embarrass him, for you will bear a sin if you cause him that embarrassment. This applies in private, and how much more so is it forbidden to embarrass him in public. By causing embarrassment, not only is one not having any positive effect on the sinner, but it is instead causing the person to sin even more, since he will not accept the rebuke due to the embarrassment he received, and it also causes more conflict. Thus the verse also implies that the one who embarrasses will bear the responsibility for the additional sins that he causes.

However, in the event that one is wronged by someone who is very boorish or mentally disturbed, it is pious behavior not to admonish the offender or mention the matter at all, and it is better to forgive him totally without bearing any ill feelings. The main concern is that such people will not take correction, and are instead likely to maintain feelings of hate for those who rebuke them.

From the outset, a person's wrongdoings should not be publicized. The prohibition of evil gossip and talebearing applies when it is the intention of the gossiper to harm another person's body or possessions, or to embarrass him with his words, or even when he simply wants to publicize a matter and has pleasure from doing this to denigrate the person whom it is about. It is, however, permissible to relate a prohibited or negative action committed by a person, privately to someone whom it is proper to tell, who will then be able to influence the wayward person to act in a proper way. This sharing of information is only permitted on the condition that it is done in a way which shows that the intention for doing so is only for the good of the wrongdoer. Nevertheless, when an evil person is a danger to others, it is permissible to publicize his evil character and his evil deeds, if the intention is so that other people will be warned about him and will take care not be harmed by him.[237]

---

[237] *Chofetz Chayim, Laws of Evil Speech*, ch. 4; *The Divine Code, 2nd Edition*, Part V, topics 8:7-8.

Chapter 6

LOVING OTHER PEOPLE AND RESPECTING OTHER PEOPLE

It is a moral injunction that one may not hate someone in his heart. Nor may one do or say anything that would degrade or belittle someone in order to embarrass him. It is also forbidden to curse anyone or speak evil about someone.[238]

One who gains honor through degrading another person does not have a share in the World to Come, and the same applies for one who deliberately embarrasses someone in public (to the point that the person's face changes color).[239] Instead, one should guard other people's honor as he would his own.

These rules of upright behavior are included in the universal "Golden Rule" that was stated by the great sage Hillel: "That which is hateful to you, do not do to another person."[240] Likewise, it is stated in the Torah, "... love your fellow as yourself; I am the Lord."[241]

A pious person will only speak about someone with mention of his praise, and constantly looks upon others favorably.[242]

As a part of the prohibition against hating others, that same verse begins: "You shall not take revenge or bear a grudge ..."

What is meant by "taking revenge"? Person A asks, "Lend me your hatchet [for example]. Person B responds, "I refuse to lend it to you." On the following day, Person B [who refused] needs to borrow a sickle. He asks Person A, "Lend me your sickle." Person A responds, "Just as you did not lend to me, I will not lend to you." This is considered to be taking revenge, and is an evil trait. Instead, one

---

[238] All of those injunctions also apply to what one feels and says about himself. Just as a person must treat others with respect, he must also treat himself with self-respect, at least on account of the "image of God" that he has within himself.

[239] Maimonides, *Laws of Personal Development* 6:3,8.

[240] Tractate *Shabbos* 31a.

[241] Leviticus 19:18.

[242] See *Ethics of the Fathers* 1:6; Maimonides, *Laws of Personal Development* 5:7.

should help others with a full heart, without making reprisals against them for wrongs they did to him in the past.

What is meant by "bearing a grudge"? Person A asked Person B, "Lend me your hatchet [for example]," and Person B was not willing to do so. On the following day, Person B asks Person A, "Lend me your sickle." Person A tells him, "Here, it is. I am lending it to you. I am not like you, who would not lend to me, nor am I paying you back for what you did." A person who acts in this manner is bearing a grudge. Instead, one should wipe such a matter from his heart and not bring it to mind. Therefore, when an unhelpful person comes asking for help, one should give it to him with a full heart, without thinking of being wronged in the past, because holding a grudge can lead to the possibility of seeking revenge.

Following these directives is the proper way, which permits a stable social environment (and healthy trade and commerce) to be established among people.[243]

This proper behavior was shown by the righteous man Joseph. Even though his brothers sold him as a slave to Egypt, he did not take revenge; on the contrary, he returned them favors, as the Torah relates, "Joseph said to them, 'Now do not fear; I will sustain you and your small children.' And he comforted them and spoke to their hearts."[244]

The above directives are the correct path of wise people. Beyond this, the pious trait of loving others was the exceptional quality of Aaron the High Priest, as it says in *Ethics of the Fathers*: "Hillel said: 'Be of the disciples of Aaron, loving peace and pursuing peace, loving your fellow creatures and bringing them near to Torah.' "[245] Although there is no injunction for a Noahide to bring other Gentiles closer to Torah, as there is for Jews, it is nevertheless clear from the example of Abraham that one should draw others to the truth of the One God, and to ways of behaving that befit the Godly image in every person.

What was Aaron's method of pursuing peace? When he saw two people arguing, he would approach each one without the other's knowledge, and would tell him, "See how your colleague is remorseful

---

[243] Maimonides, *Laws of Personal Development* 7:7-8.

[244] Genesis 50:21.

[245] *Ethics of the Fathers* 1:12.

and feels bad for sinning against you? He asked me to approach you to ask you to forgive him." Through Aaron's method, both colleagues would approach and embrace each other.

How did he love the creatures and draw them close to Torah? When he knew of a person who committed a sin, he would approach him with a pleasant demeanor, greet him and get friendly with him. The sinner would become embarrassed and think to himself, "If this righteous person would know my sinful actions, he would surely distance himself from me, and wouldn't even look at me or speak to me. But since he must be thinking that I'm an honorable person, I will change my ways in order to be fitting to truly grow close to this righteous person." In this manner, the sinner would repent and change his ways for the good. Regarding this practice, God says, "In peace and uprightness he [Aaron] went with Me, and he brought back many away from iniquity."[246,247]

In summary, the level of a wise person in regard to these traits is that he does not hate others, even if they have wronged him, but rather forgives them and does not take revenge, and acts with peace to all. Beyond this, it is a trait of a pious person to pursue peace and love all creations, to go out of one's way to do favors for another, and to be swift to extend kindness and help to anyone who needs it.

---

[246] Malachi 2:6.

[247] *Avot D'Rabbi Natan*, quoted in *Pirush Ha'Rambam* and Rav Ovadiah of Bartenura on the Mishnah *Avot (Ethics of the Fathers)*, ibid.

Chapter 7

THE CARE THAT A WISE AND RIGHTEOUS PERSON MUST TAKE IN SPEAKING

It is forbidden for a person to embarrass another, even if only with speech, or call another with a name that is embarrassing to him, or speak before him about a matter that is embarrassing to him.[248] The sages said: "A person who embarrasses a colleague in public (to the point that his face changes color) does not have a share in the World to Come."[249] Abiding by this manner of conduct, Tamar did not wish to publicize the fact that Judah had conceived with her, even though doing so would have saved her from a death sentence. She said, "Better that I should die and not embarrass him in public."[250]

It is forbidden to spread gossip. Who is a gossiper? One who collects information and then goes from person to person, saying: "This is what so and so said;" "This is what I heard about so and so." Even if the statements are true, this sin can bring about destruction in the world, and can cause the death of many people, God forbid.[251] Consider what happened because Doeg the Edomite gossiped to King Saul about the Jewish priests in the town of Nov, which caused of all those priests to be killed.[252] For causing this, Doeg was cursed by King David, and died at half his intended life span.[253]

The gossiper is not the only one who sins when he spreads his words. The one who listens to the gossip commits a greater sin, since he enables and encourages the gossip to be said to him.[254] Therefore it is forbidden to listen to the gossip, unless he perceives that it is crucial to take heed of the information being relayed, and that is why he listens.[255]

---

[248] Maimonides, *Laws of Personal Development*, ch. 6.

[249] Tractates *Bava Metzia* 59a and *Arachin* 16b.

[250] Tractate *Sotah* 10b.

[251] Maimonides, *Laws of Personal Development*, ch. 7.

[252] I Samuel, ch. 22.

[253] Tractate *Sanhedrin* 106b; this is what David wrote about in Psalms 55:24.

[254] Maimonides, ibid. This applies to both simple gossip and evil speech.

[255] *Shulchan Aruch HaRav* 156:10.

There is a much more serious sin than simple gossip, and that is *lashon hara* (in Hebrew, translated literally as "evil speech"),[256] i.e., relating negative things about another person. This apples even if the things said about the other person are true, and whether or not the person who is being spoken about is present at the time. If saying something about a person would bring any kind of harm to him or his property, or even if it would only embarrass, annoy, or frighten him if he knew it was said, it is considered to be *lashon hara*.

As above, the one who listens to and accepts someone's evil speech commits a greater sin, because he enables and encourages it to be spread. (One is only allowed to listen to it if he perceives it is crucial to take heed of the information being relayed, for safety or well-being).

It is common to think, "How have I done any serious wrong? I only related something, or overheard something." Therefore, everyone is obligated to distance himself exceedingly from this sin, for these are ways that the evil inclination entices one to participate in it, by speaking or listening.

It is forbidden to sit among a gathering of people who regularly relate *lashon hara* and gossip. If one has the misfortune to be found amongst such a gathering and cannot leave (or cannot be successful in protesting to them to stop the sin they are committing), one should at least not be involved in their talk at all, and not show any approval or satisfaction with this talk, and be steadfast in not accepting that there is truth to any of the gossip being related about other people.

A pious person will avoid gossip and *lashon hara* to the utmost, and will also be careful in all matters of speech. One should not even be involved with the "the dust of *lashon hara*." This is the expression the sages used to describe negative implications that are spoken about someone, without relating anything specifically, such as: "Who will tell so-and-so that he should always act the way he is acting now?" or "Don't talk about so-and-so; I don't want to say what happened!" or the like. The reason is because these insinuating comments will bring others to speak about that person in a negative way, and eventually it will result in evil speech – *lashon hara*.

---

[256] The details of this prohibition are presented in *The Divine Code*, Part V (The Prohibition of Murder and Injury), ch. 8.

Similarly, it is also considered to be "dust of *lashon hara*" when someone speaks favorably about a person in the presence of his enemies, for this will surely prompt them to rebut the praise and speak disparagingly about the person. One should also not thank or praise someone loudly in public, for those who overhear may be drawn to find ways to take advantage of the person. In this regard, King Solomon said:[257] "He who blesses his friend in a loud voice early in the morning [with loud thanks for favors he did the night before], it shall be considered a curse for him."[258]

One should avoid gatherings of frivolous people who sit and speak words of folly, and this certainly applies if they habitually use profanity. Being involved with such things removes a person from the world.[259]

Flattering other people should be avoided, for flattery is false and deceiving, and it is improper behavior for an upright person. One who is fearful of a sinner and therefore flatters him does not have proper fear of God, and deserves punishment for doing this. However, if someone is in serious danger from a sinner, and he can escape from the danger by using flattery, it is permitted to do so.[260]

Beyond everything that is presented in this chapter, a pious person also endeavors to use his words and influence to promote matters which help establish a moral society. The foremost way to accomplish this is by establishing or supporting institutions and a society overall in which the Torah's universal lessons of wisdom and good behavior are taught, to students who will go in that path. (And if one is able, he himself should be involved in teaching this, for the sages encouraged pious people to "raise up many disciples."[261]) For if someone brings many people to be meritorious, then in this merit, no sin will come

---

[257] Proverbs 27:14.

[258] Maimonides, *Laws of Personal Development* 7:4; Rashi on Proverbs, ibid.; Tractate *Arachin* 16a.

[259] See Maimonides, *Laws of Personal Development* 7:6. See also Rashi's commentary on *Ethics of the Fathers* 3:10.

[260] *Shulchan Aruch HaRav, Orach Chayim* 156:18.

[261] *Ethics of the Fathers* 1:1.

about through him. But if someone brings many people to sin, then he will not be given the opportunity to repent for his sins. In support of this teaching, the sages brought these prime examples:[262]

> Moses was meritorious and caused many people to be meritorious, and therefore the merit of the many is attributed to him, as it is stated, "He [Moses] performed the righteousness of God and His ordinances with Israel."[263] Jeroboam the son of Nevat sinned and caused many people to sin, and therefore the sin of the many is attributed to him; as is stated, "For the sins of Jeroboam, which he sinned and caused Israel to sin."[264]

---

[262] Ibid. 5:17.

[263] Deuteronomy 33:21, as explained in *Sifri* 33:21 – the Children of Israel observed God's righteous ordinances as a result of the positive influence they received from Moses.

[264] I Kings 15:30.

Chapter 8

RESPECTING PEOPLE WHO SUFFER MISFORTUNES; HONORING PARENTS; HONORING ONE'S SPOUSE; EDUCATING CHILDREN

Although it is moral to respect all people, including strangers, there are specific people whom one must respect more than usual, either due to their need for more care and friendship because of their unfortunate situation, or due to one's greater obligation to them, such as parents, teachers, close friends, or one who has done the person a favor.

A wise or pious person who sees an unfortunate person or invalid should make certain to help and encourage the person in any way possible, whether monetarily, with good advice, or uplifting the afflicted person's broken spirit with caring words and attention, more so than one would normally help the average person.

One should be careful not to speak callously to a distressed person.[265] For example: one may not speak to an ill person about matters of his health that are distressful to him; if a person has had a financial loss, one should not pain him by speaking about his business ventures. God made a covenant about the cries of the deprived, that He will bring retribution on those who cause them to suffer – as it says, "For if he shall cry out to Me, I will surely hear his cry."[266] If anyone harasses them with hurtful words and intends to distress and pain them, and therefore they cry out, they are answered. God hears the cry of the poor, and hearkens to the cry of the downtrodden – as it is stated, "To the poor person who is with you ... if he cries out to Me [that someone has pained or oppressed him], I shall listen, for I am compassionate."[267]

One should greet every person with a gracious and respectful countenance. By doing so, one implies that the other person is important and befitting to receive the greeting. One who turns away and does not greet others, or does not answer their greetings, implies

---

[265] See Maimonides, *Laws of Personal Development* 6:10; *Laws of Gifts to the Poor* 7:2; *Laws of Selling* 14:12-13,18.

[266] Exodus 22:22.

[267] Exodus 22:24,26.

that they are not befitting or important in his eyes, and this will embarrass a person greatly.

An upright person should not be ungracious, but rather should recognize the favors that another does for him. Ungraciousness is a bad trait which only causes evil to a person, for other people distance themselves from one who is ungracious, and they do not want companionship with such a person. Rather, one should always thank others appropriately, remembering and mentioning the good they did for him, and teach himself to do favors for others in their time of need.

It is most important to give special honor and be gracious to one's parents and grandparents. A wise person will also honor his older brothers and sisters. The following are some of the ways of moral conduct in respecting a father and mother.

Honoring parents is commanded in the Torah[268] – as it is stated, "Honor your father and mother,"[269] and, "A man should fear his mother and father."[270] What is meant by fear of one's parents? One should not stand or sit in his parents' established places, nor argue with them, nor contradict their words in their presence in (regard to mundane matters).[271] A person should not call either of his parents by their first names, but should rather call them by respectful terms for "Father" and "Mother" in accordance with the community's custom. What is considered honoring one's parents? When it becomes difficult for one's parents to shop for themselves, he should bring them proper food, drink, and clothing (paid for from the parents' resources, if those are adequate). One should assist his parents as needed, and stand

---

[268] This is one of the 613 commandments for Jews. See *Likkutei Sichot* vol. 5, p. 154: it is possible that honoring parents is an intellectual obligation for Gentiles just like giving charity is, for it is necessary for the establishment of a proper society and proper laws (*dinim* in Hebrew). It is obvious that a Gentile is at least forbidden to embarrass his parents, since it is against logical human respect.

[269] Exodus 20:12.

[270] Leviticus 19:3.

[271] Regarding the precepts and basic principles of Torah, a person who knows he is correct should nevertheless guard himself from falling into heated arguments with his parents, and keep in mind that "a gentle reply turns away wrath, but a distressing word stirs up anger" (Proverbs 15:1). See fn. 275.

respectfully before them. One should also honor his parents with his words, and it should be recognized from his way of talking to them that he respects them highly.[272]

One who curses, degrades or embarrasses a parent is a sinner and will be punished by Heaven for this sin, as Ham and his son Canaan were punished for disgracing Ham's father, Noah.[273] Therefore, even if one's parents vex him, he should remain silent and not embarrass them.

One is obligated to honor his wife, and concern himself for her welfare. The sages said, "A man's house is blessed solely due to his wife."[274] When there is peace, love and trust between a couple, blessing and success shine in the house. By the same token, a wife is obligated to honor her husband.

As part of the due respect between the couple, they should consult between themselves in conducting the affairs of the home, including the raising and education of their children, with true partnership.[275] As a general statement, the sages said, "Who is honorable? One who honors the creations"[276] (i.e., he even honors people whose only apparent praise is that they are creations of God). Surely, then, spouses must honor each other, both in private and in public.[277]

Even when a husband and wife are intimate with each other in private, they should be careful to behave modestly in God's eyes, and not act brazenly like dogs that copulate in the street. (Previously we

---

[272] Maimonides, *Laws of the Rebellious Ones*, ch. 6.

[273] Genesis 9:22-25, and Rashi's explanation there. See also *Pirkei Rebbe Eliezer* ch. 23, and Ibn Ezra on Deuteronomy 21:13.

[274] Tractate *Bava Metzia* 59a.

[275] This assumes that both parents are believers in the One God. If one of the parents is an idol worshiper or an atheist, the God-fearing parent should make every effort in a respectful way to be the decider of the religious and moral education of the children, in accordance with Torah principles for righteous Gentiles.

[276] *Ethics of the Fathers* 4:1.

[277] If one spouse dishonors the other in public, that is like a person who degrades his own self in public. Especially, a man who dishonors his wife should be considered dishonorable in the eyes of other people. A spouse who cannot honor the other partner should seek the advice of upright friends, or a professional marriage counselor.

explained the moral lesson that can be inferred from the Noahide prohibition of forbidden relations, in "The Gate of Serving God," Chapter 2). The couple should not speak obscene nonsense, even in their intimate conversations between themselves.[278] (In fact, a person should never use profanity, even in the privacy of his own home, for God is always listening.)

One should not be ungracious to God, and should instead give thanks to Him and praise Him for all the good He has bestowed upon him, especially for the greatest gift God gives a person – his children.

Both parents are obligated to be scrupulous regarding the raising of their children so that they should grow up in a proper manner: going in the ways of God, with good character traits and proper views that are consistent with Torah values about the world and their own lives. Parents should be vigilant that their children do not befriend anyone who would have bad influence on them.

It is obligatory for a person to ensure that his sons and daughters are each taught a useful trade, commensurate with their individual abilities, so they will be able to live honorably and not have to depend on public assistance. The sages said, "One who does not teach his son a trade, is as if he taught him to be a thief."[279]

It is proper for one to give money to his sons and daughters, even if they are past the age of maturity, in a way that directs them in an upright path and helps them to become self-supportive. The sages said, "One who gives money to his sons and daughters *to learn a trade*, and similarly one who provides food to his father and his mother, is included among those who give charity.[280]

God praised Abraham for guiding his children and his followers in this way, as God said about him: "For I have known him, because he commands his children and his household after him, that they shall keep the path of God, to perform charity and justice, so that God will bring upon Abraham that which He spoke about him."[281] This refers to the promises and blessings which God gave to Abraham.

---

[278] Maimonides, *Laws of Personal Development* 5:4.

[279] Tractate *Kiddushin* 29a.

[280] Maimonides, *Laws of Charity* 10:16.

[281] Genesis 18:19.

Chapter 9

CHARITY AND ACTS OF KINDNESS

It is explained in *The Divine Code*[282] that Gentiles are obligated to give charity and do acts of kindness, to be concerned for the welfare of the poor and unfortunate, and give to them aid. One who gives proper charity is acting piously; he is acting in accordance with the image of God in which he is created, for this is also the conduct of the Creator, Blessed be He. The sages said, "Just as the Holy One, blessed be He, is called Merciful, so should you be merciful; just as He is called Gracious, so should you be gracious ..."[187]

The focal point of kindness is giving charity to the poor. It is the hallmark of a pious person to be charitable with the needy, and for a Gentile this is truly pious behavior, for he is going beyond the measure of the law in his relationship with both God and his fellowman.

One who gives charity to a poor person should not do so unpleasantly or with his face down. Instead, he should give the charity with a pleasant countenance and cheerfulness, yet commiserating with the poor person's troubles – as Job said, "Did I not weep for those who face difficult times; did not my soul feel sorrow for the destitute?"[283] This is an attribute of God – as it is stated, "So said [God,] the High and Exalted One, ... 'I abide in exaltedness and holiness, but I am with the [people who are] despondent and lowly of spirit, to revive the spirit of the lowly and to revive the heart of the despondent.' "[284] If one is asked by a poor person for charity and has nothing to give, he should conciliate him with words. One should not scold a poor person or raise one's voice against him and shout,[285] because his heart is broken and crushed, and therefore God is with him – as it is stated, "a contrite and broken heart, God, You do not disdain."[286]

---

[282] In Part I (Foundations of the Faith), topics 3:8-9.

[283] Job 30:25.

[284] Isaiah 57:15.

[285] Maimonides, *Laws of Gifts to the Poor* 10:4-5. Although it is questionable if we can say this is forbidden for a Gentile, it surely shows bad character.

[286] Psalms 51:19.

A pious person who gives charity should not seek to be honored for doing so. It is admirable to give charity secretly, so that the poor recipient will not feel shamed. There is no greater giver of charity than God, Who gives existence to the whole world at every moment, and He does so secretly, hiding His Presence from the mortal recipients of His kindness.[287]

The highest level of charity occurs when a person supports someone who has fallen into poverty by giving him a present or a loan that he will use to achieve a steady livelihood. Giving money is not even required, if the poor person is given the advice he needs, or a job or a partnership, that will bring him to be self-sufficient. It is a great merit to help others find work that will sustain them comfortably and honorably.[288]

Why is this greater than any other form of charity? A poor person who accepts handouts is embarrassed by doing this, but for one who receives help or a loan that allows him to begin an occupation, he has been saved from falling to that level. Instead, he feels honorable and not disgraced, because he will be able to repay the loan, and he will be supporting himself. Therefore, one who gives help in this manner has not only given charity, but also honor as well, and he does kindness by sparing the recipient from embarrassment and degradation.

Also included in doing this level of charity and kindness is one who finds a successful match between a man and a woman to join in marriage, and then helps them to establish their home.

Other traits of kindness that God displayed in the Torah are:[289] clothing the naked (for Adam and Hava), visiting the sick (for Abraham), comforting the bereaved (for Isaac), and burying the dead (for Moses). God also demonstrated the kindness of providing for the needs of a new couple (Adam and Hava) in their marriage.[290]

---

[287] *Igeret Hakodesh* (Tanya, Part IV), ch. 17.

[288] Maimonides, *Laws of Gifts to the Poor* 10:7.

[289] Tractate *Sotah* 14a.

[290] See Tractates *Berachot* 61a and *Bava Batra* 75a, and *Midrash Rabbah Bereishit* 8:13.

Inviting guests was a main characteristic and method of kindness displayed by Abraham. He would bring in people who were traveling through the desert, and give them sumptuous food and drink (and accommodations if they needed), and he would then escort them on their way.[291] The following episode teaches that hospitality to guests is a greater spiritual accomplishment than receiving God's Presence:[292] The Torah relates, "And God appeared to him [Abraham] ... and he saw; and behold, three men were standing before him ... and he ran toward them [to invite them]."[293] Abraham was sitting in communion with God, yet he asked God to wait for him while he ran to invite the "men" (who were angels in disguise) to be his guests.[294]

One who escorts a guest who is leaving on his way has done a greater deed than one who has invited him in and fed him. The sages said: one who does not escort a guest on his way is as if he had shed blood."[295] The cited measure for escorting is at least four cubits (6-8 feet) outside of the home.[296]

When a person observes a joyous event and wishes to make a celebration feast, he should also provide from it food for the local needy and unfortunate people, so that God will also be joining in the joy of the occasion. Conversely, one who locks his house and feasts with his family, without feeding poor people, is not rejoicing with a righteous happiness, but rather he is only rejoicing in the satisfaction of his innards, and this is a disgraceful trait.[297]

---

[291] See the excerpt on p. 5 above, from Tractate *Sotah* 10b.

[292] Tractate *Shabbat* 127a.

[293] Genesis 18:1-2.

[294] Hospitality is another of God's traits that one should emulate, as expounded by Shelah, *Parshat Vayeira, Ner Mitzvah* (2nd par.): "The Holy One, Blessed be He, extends hospitality to guests ... if not for God's hospitality at every moment, then all of existence would cease to exist. This means that all the inhabitants of the world are like guests of God. A person is like one who has come to lodge. We are visitors here, and God hosts us."

[295] Maimonides, *Laws of Mourning* 14:2.

[296] Tractate *Sotah* 45b.

[297] Maimonides, *Laws of Resting on the Holy Days* 6:18.

Anyone who gives food and drink to the poor and orphans at his table merits that if he will need to call out to God, then God will answer him, and he will derive pleasure from Him – as it is stated,[298] "Surely you should slice a piece of your bread for the hungry, and bring the moaning poor to your home ... Then you will call and God will respond; you will cry out and He will say, 'Here I am.' "[299]

The culmination of all one's good traits is expressed in the trait of doing kindness for others, and it is the correct trait that rises above all the others.

It is a pious trait and a wise path for a person to be merciful and pursue righteousness, and not be overbearing, even towards one's subordinates. One should not pain them or cause them trouble. The early righteous ones would give their servants a portion of every food they would eat, and would feed their animals and servants before they themselves began to eat. This behavior is in accordance with the verse, "Indeed, as the eyes of servants are turned to the hand of their masters, as the eyes of a maidservant to the hand of her mistress, so are our eyes turned to the Lord our God, until He will be gracious to us. Be gracious to us, Lord, be gracious to us ..."[300]

One should not yell or get angry at one's subordinates, but should rather speak with them gently and listen to their grievances. Job strived to act in this manner – as it says, "If I ever spurned justice for my servants and maidservants when they contended with me; then what could I do when God would rise up [to examine my ways], and when He would make an accounting of me, what could I answer Him? Did not the One Who made me in the womb make him [my servant] too, and did not One form us both in the womb?"[301] This surely applies to one's interaction with other people, and it reflects a trait of God that we should emulate – as it says,[302] "The Lord is good to all, and His mercies are over all His works."[303]

---

[298] Isaiah 58:7,9.

[299] Maimonides, *Laws of Gifts to the Poor* 10:16.

[300] Psalms 123:2-3.

[301] Job 31:13-15.

[302] Psalms 145:9.

[303] Maimonides, *Laws Governing Slaves* 9:8.

The sages said, "Similar to the measure that one acts, it is measured to him;"[304] i.e., in the same way a person acts in his own wrongdoings, and in the way he acts toward others, God acts correspondingly toward him. This is said regarding a person's wrong behavior, and it applies even more so to the correct behavior of a pious and wise person. One who has mercy on others will receive mercy from God; one who forgives and pardons others will also receive God's forgiveness and pardon; and one who judges others favorably will be judged favorably. This will be granted to him, measure for measure, even if he retains some wrong tendencies.

---

[304] Tractate *Sotah* 8b, 9b.

The Sixth Gate: The Gate of Being Tested by God

Chapter 1

Why God Tests People

A pious person who serves the Blessed and Exalted God will know that part of one's service is withstanding tests. Each person has a different Divine service than the next, as each person's views and character are different from the next person. Likewise, each person has different tests than the next, but certainly, every person does have his own challenges and tests.

The sages said, "There is no wise person like one who withstands a test," meaning that one who was tested, and withstood the test, is certainly a truly wise person.

It is known in all areas of authentic analysis that a theory alone is not considered absolute and reliable truth, and only a practical test can determine the authenticity of the theory. The same applies to a test of a person's true character – of one's good traits, faith and trust in God. A person's idea or views cannot guarantee the truth of his traits. Rather, that which is put to a practical test will have a degree of certainty. The greater the degree of the test that the person is put through and withstands, the greater the degree of the proof of the truthfulness of the person's traits.

Likewise, the verse states, "For the Lord your God is putting you to proof, to know whether you love the Lord your God with all your heart and with all your soul."[305] A challenge refines a person and his faith, and humbles the heart, and thereby brings a person closer to God. Therefore, in truth, a test is a great benefit for a person."[306]

A main part of a challenge is the question the person will ask and wonder: "Why has this challenge and hardship befallen me?"

This is the essence of a challenge – to determine whether the person believes that there is a certain service and mission that God has assigned for him, or if he does not believe that he is obligated in this

---

[305] Deuteronomy 13:4.
[306] See Nachmanidies on Genesis 22:1.

service, and therefore reaches the question: "Why is God setting me up with this pain?"

The sages taught, "One is obligated to say a blessing [to God] over bad tidings, just as he says a blessing over good tidings."[307] For the truth is that whatever God does in the world is good – as it says, "Is it not from the mouth of the Most High that evil and good emanate?"[308] This means that God is always in full control and everything is from Him, and no evil happens. Rather, our perception of an event as bad is only based on our shortsightedness and limited understanding. The truth is that what we perceive as a bad event is in essence a kindness from God, and it is such a powerful good that it cannot be openly revealed, for it cannot yet be grasped by the severely limited ability and frame of reference of our human minds.[309]

The general nature of tests from God can be divided into two categories: a test of attraction to spiritual evil (a temptation to sin), or a test of physical hardship:

1. A test of spiritual evil comes from one's evil inclination, which endeavors to make a person sin. Included in this category are a person's challenges from seeing other individuals sinning, or seeing his general society being engaged in forbidden activities. One is drawn to be like them and joined with them by acting in concert with their sinful ways.

Part of this test comes from the questions: "Why are evil people successful? Why does God hide His face from showing truth and justice in the world? Why does He not grant success to righteous people, or punish and hinder the evildoers?"

Another part of this test is that many people endeavor to attain much honor and riches, yet they do not know how to use these things for good and correct purposes; instead, they use them for negative ends.

2. One can be tested by challenges in life – the hardships of earning a livelihood, or physical problems or loss of loved ones, or natural disasters, or any other types of tribulations that come upon people.

---

[307] Mishnah *Berachot* 9:5.

[308] Lamentations 3:38.

[309] *Likkutei Amarim* (Tanya, Part I), ch. 26.

These are all difficult tests, and the question arises in the person's heart: "Why is this happening to me?"

When a person has difficulty during a challenge, it may go against his nature to stand strong in his faith and trust in the Creator, and at the same time, his evil inclination brings him to question whether he is going in a correct path or not in his service of God. Furthermore, when one's faculties are weakened by troubles, it is hard to be strong-minded.

The Godly purpose in any of the abovementioned tests is to uplift the person. Who is a greater example for us than Abraham? He was the first and only person to discover the One True God completely on his own. He then contended for many years against all the world's idolatrous societies to convince them that there is only one God who directs everything, and that all idols and idol worship are false. Yet this righteous and pious person was tested by God with ten harsh challenges. Abraham withstood them all, and with this God showed how greatly he loved Him.[310]

A person may wrongly think, "Perhaps I am not capable and fitting to do the service which God commands for me, and therefore God is afflicting me with hardships." The person should instead ask, "If God Himself testified in the Torah about Abraham's right and correct path and pureness of heart, then why did he receive these ten bitter and harsh tests?"

Rather, through being tested, Abraham reached much loftier spiritual levels than he could have reached on his own. Because of God's love for Abraham, He tested him and raised him above his worldly limitations and natural traits, through leading him to refine his conduct in the face of great adversity. God did this to demonstrate to Abraham and the people of all subsequent generations, how true were his faith and trust and his commitment to following the One God's instructions in all of his ways.

Maimonides identified Abraham's ten tests as the following difficulties that he faced[311] (his name was Abram until God changed it to Abraham in Genesis 17:5):

---

[310] *Ethics of the Fathers* 5:3.
[311] *Pirush Ha'Mishnayos L'Rambam,* ibid.

1. God's command to Abram to leave his homeland and travel to sojourn in another country, without telling him where that would be, as God said to him, "Go for yourself from your land, from your birthplace, and from your father's house, to the land that I will show you."[312]

2. The famine that occurred in the Land of Canaan when he arrived there – as it says, "And there was a famine in the land, and Abram descended to Egypt to sojourn there, for the famine was severe in the land."[313] This happened despite the fact that God had promised him, "And I will make you into a great nation ..."[314] He was faced with the exact opposite of what God had told him – he became impoverished and afflicted by the famine in the land that God led him to, and this was an immense test.

3. The oppression he suffered from the Egyptians when they took his wife Sarai (whom God later renamed as Sarah) and brought her to the pharaoh.[315]

4. His battle with the armies of the four kings who kidnapped his nephew Lot.[316]

5. Heeding Sarai's instructions to take her handmaid Hagar as a second wife, after Sarai's sterility continued,[317] even though he was promised by God that he would have a child in his old age.[318]

6. His circumcision at the old age of 99, which God commanded him to do.[319]

7. The oppression he suffered when Abimelech, the Philistine king of Gerar, took Sarah away from him.[320]

---

[312] Genesis 12:1.

[313] Ibid., 12:10.

[314] Ibid., 12:2.

[315] Ibid., 12:15.

[316] Ibid., 14:14-15.

[317] Ibid., 16:1-3.

[318] Ibid., 15:4.

[319] Ibid., 17:24.

[320] Ibid., 20:2.

8. Being impelled by God to follow his wife Sarah's instructions to send away his concubine Hagar into the desert, along with Ishmael, his son whom he had with her.[321]

9. Being instructed by God at that time to distance himself from Ishmael, despite his fatherly love for him – as God commanded him, "Do not be distressed over the lad ..."[322] The preceding verse testifies how disturbing this matter was to Abraham ("The matter greatly distressed Abraham, regarding his son"), yet he still followed Sarah's instructions as God told him to do, and expelled Hagar and Ishmael.

10. Swiftly following God's request that he offer Isaac, his most beloved son, as a sacrifice to Him.[323]

One should contemplate that as much as Abraham was pious and trusted God, and had faith in Him, he was still tested repeatedly by such difficult tests as these, which the average person would have no power to withstand. Why did God test him this way, so many times? It was because He wanted to demonstrate His love for Abraham. He wanted to show all people (and Abraham himself as well) how close he was to God, to the extent that he cleaved to God with all his might under difficult circumstances. Abraham did not weigh any nor all of his tribulations and challenging experiences – whatever they were – against his faith and trust in God.

---

[321] Ibid., 21:10-12.

[322] Ibid., 21:12.

[323] Ibid., 22:1-10.

Chapter 2

A TROUBLE OR TRIBULATION THAT COMES
UPON SOCIETY OR AN INDIVIDUAL

From the text of Maimonides, *Laws of Fasts:*[324]

"... when a difficulty arises [which affects a community], and the people cry out [to God in prayer to save them] ... everyone will realize that [the difficulty] occurred because of their evil conduct ... This [realization, and their repentance and prayers] will cause the removal of this difficulty from among them.

Conversely, should the people fail to cry out [to God] ... and instead say, 'What has happened to us is [merely a natural phenomenon, as is] customary in the world,' this [sin of denial] is added on to their wrongdoings."

What is their additional sin, in the second case? By ignoring the message of the difficulty that was originally sent to them from God, as a sign from Heaven, they are portraying the acts of God in the world as random and therefore cruel (God forbid), and they deny the truth of His ways (even though this was clearly taught by all the prophets of the Hebrew Bible). Therefore, measure for measure, such a community is liable to receive additional suffering, as punishment for their sins.

A trouble that comes upon a community results from their sins as a community. For example, the community in general may be accepting of a particular serious sin or immoral behavior that many of the people there commit regularly as their normal way of acting. Some examples in the Hebrew Bible are: the generations of the Flood and the Tower of Babel;[325] the metropolis around Sodom in the days of Abraham;[326] the city of Nineveh in the days of the prophet Jonah;[327] and the Land of Israel in the days of the prophet Joel.[328] If the people admit their wrongdoing, stop the sinful behavior that caused this, and collectively

---

[324] *Laws of Fasts* 1:2-3.

[325] Genesis 6:1-5,11 and 17:1-9, respectively.

[326] Which practiced cruelty and sexual immorality; see Gen. 18:20, 19:4,5,9.

[327] Where the people indulged in theft and extortion; see Jonah 1: 2, 3:5-10.

[328] When the people sinned through idolatry and drunkenness; Joel 1:5, 2:27.

repent, they will be forgiven, and the trouble will be averted as God did for the people of Nineveh,[329] or removed as in the time of Joel.

This is not the same as in the case of trouble that occurs to an individual. If it is God's will and wisdom that an individual person is to receive distress, then if he prays and repents and fixes his ways – and especially if other individuals also pray for God to help this person – then it is possible that God in His mercy will remove the trouble. But it is also possible that God in His wisdom made it a firm decree that will not be removed, even if this person prays and repents to the utmost of his (limited) ability.[330] Even if his prayer is not fully granted, God may ease his trouble from what it would have been otherwise. Regardless, it is still obligatory to endeavor to better one's ways, repent, and pray to God to be saved from the distress, because in either case, the person needs to draw closer to God through all of that Divine service for his own benefit. The merit he earns from doing this will bring him a reward from God, either during his physical life or in his spiritual afterlife. At the same time, by enduring his troubles with faith that it is all for the best, they will provide an amount of atonement for his sins. It is a fundamental principle that trouble is administered by God to cleanse a person's soul,[331] and although it is temporarily painful, this knowledge itself should help the person to endure the pain and remain thankful to God for the blessings that he has.

On a very simple level, one can understand this concept based on an analogy with the beneficial function of physical pain that accompanies an injury or illness. If a person did not feel pain, he would not know that he was injured or sick, and he would not realize that he must act as soon as possible to get the proper treatment or begin a healthier lifestyle, in order to preserve his live and health. The purpose of God's creation of the bodily function of feeling pain is not for the sake of the pain itself, God forbid, and not so that it should continue without

---

[329] Jonah 3:1-10.

[330] Although it may be that on his limited spiritual level, the afflicted person will not have the ability to bring a change in God's decree, it is possible that a very righteous and pious person (a *tzaddik*), who is on a much higher spiritual level, may be able to see the situation from a higher perspective and successfully bless the person that the affliction will be removed.

[331] See Psalms 89:31-35.

relief. Rather, it is the body's "alarm system" to notify the person that his body needs healing. Likewise, troubles and pain also serve as a spiritual "alarm system" to alert the person to honestly examine and improve his ways, and that God is desiring for the person to come closer to Him with faith and repentance.

A person's troubles also serve as a spiritual test. They may be administered by God to challenge one's faith in Him, in order to demonstrate whether or not the person will love and respect Him and trust in Him under difficult circumstances (as exemplified by the ten tests of Abraham listed in the previous chapter). The foremost source where this great lesson is taught is the Book of Job, which should be read and meditated upon. The understanding that a challenge or trouble comes from God for a good purpose, or for a Divine purpose beyond human understanding, will enable the person to endure it, and more importantly, to use it to grow spiritually and to discover his innate strengths and abilities that previously remained hidden.

The trust and faith that everything comes from God, Who only does good, and that He is together with a person in all harsh situations, will help a person to accept his difficulties with more tranquility. (The very fact that people in the world still experience pain and suffering is due to the mystical truth that God's Divine Presence in the world, the *Shechinah*, is still suffering along with us in our temporary condition of spiritual exile and the continuing destruction of His dwelling place, the Holy Temple in Jerusalem.[332]) When a person in distress recognizes the connection he has with God's Presence, he can receive his situation with cheerfulness – as it says, "Happy is the man whom You chasten."[333] And because he knows that everything comes from God and is for his ultimate benefit, whether in this world or in his afterlife, this happiness turns his perception of his pains and troubles

---

[332] This current and final spiritual exile was caused due to sins, and when the sins will be atoned and corrected though the process of the exile, the true Messiah will come immediately and rebuild God's Holy Temple, speedily in our days. From that time on, "there will be neither famine or war, envy or competition, for good will flow in abundance; all the delights will be freely available as dust, and the occupation of the entire world will be solely to know God" (Maimonides, *Laws of Kings* 12:5).

[333] Psalms 94:12; see also Psalm 51.

into good, which is in fact the true reality of their hidden source within the Supernal Good.[334]

The Talmud tells the story of the sage Nachum Ish Gamzu, who used to say at any seemingly negative occurrence, "This too is for the good."[335] This righteous man had faith and knew that however God dealt with him, it was for his good, including even the things that sometimes seemed on a superficial level to be a bad occurrence. Through his deep faith, a seemingly disastrous occurrence that befell him was miraculously revealed as good.[336]

Even if one is not able to reach the level of accepting pain and suffering with happiness (as this is a truly lofty level that requires great refinement of the soul), he is nevertheless able to contemplate and meditate on the fact that it is in truth for the good (even though he is not yet on the level to actually see that it is). This concept in itself will help him to be strengthened despite the hardships, and will make it easier for him to endure them, despite his natural tendency to feel otherwise.

Just as all things that God does for a person are for his good, a person should know that whatever desires God puts into his heart through his evil inclination are also for the good. The evil inclination, which tries to seduce him to sin, is not part of his inner essence, but is like a bad spirit that rests in the person to test him.[337] (This mode of our existence began with the temptation and fall of Adam and Hava on

---

[334] *Igeret Hakodesh* (Tanya, Part IV), ch. 11, p. 117.

[335] Tractate *Taanit* 21a.

[336] However, it once happened that this righteous and greatly pious sage failed to provide sustenance quickly enough to a poor person, on account of which the person suddenly died of starvation. The sage thereupon accepted upon himself a decree of horrific illness and suffering, which he felt he needed to atone for his error. His disciples were aghast at his wretched state, but he wholeheartedly told them, "Woe [it would be] to me if you had not seen me in this state, for this suffering atones for me."

[337] See *Likkuei Amarim* (Tanya, Part I), ch. 8: "The evil inclination and the power [of desire] that strains after forbidden things is a demon ..."

the day of their creation in the Garden of Eden, in accordance with God's plan.[338])

It is for the benefit of a person to fight against his bad inclination and subdue and control it, for this reveals his inner powers and the image of God within him. Through this ongoing battle he will merit to become a pious servant of God, blessed be He, like a soldier who serves valiantly on the field of battle for the defense and love of his homeland. It is only through this war with one's internal evil that one can awaken his inner powers to beseech God for His help in this effort and to become ever closer to Him, as explained above regarding Abraham's tests.[339]

In the Zohar,[340] the following parable is brought for God's purpose in creating the evil inclination:

A king wanted to see if his son the prince would withstand a moral challenge and be of strong spirit and control his desires, or if he was frivolous and would succumb to licentiousness. Therefore the king commanded a most beautiful and skilled harlot to endeavor to seduce his son, while the king would be secretly watching from a hidden place. The harlot herself knows that by the command of the king, she must do her best to succeed in persuading the prince, and she has no permission from the king to reveal her mission. But in her heart she knows the truth and hopes that the prince will succeed in not being seduced by her, in order that both she and the prince will find favor in the eyes of the king. Thus she knows that if the prince proves to be upright, and she fails to succeed in her effort, she will have caused a true pleasure and benefit for the king.

---

[338] This is in accordance with the teaching from the Midrash (*Genesis Rabbah* 9:7), that at the end of the sixth day of creation, when "God saw everything that He had made and behold, it was **very** good" (Genesis 1:31), "good" refers to the good inclination, and "very good" refers to the evil inclination, for "were it not for the evil inclination, no one would build a house or have children or engage in commerce."

[339] See the writings of Rabbi Shneur Zalman of Liadi: *Likutei Torah, Bamidbar* 61b, *"Vayaas Moshe;" Torah Or* 8b, *"Mayim Rabim."*

[340] Zohar, Exodus 163a.

Likewise, the evil inclination is sent into a person's heart in this world to test him. But the forces of impurity in the spiritual realm, from which the evil inclination is drawn down, know the truth: that their inner purpose in God's plan will be fulfilled if the person overcomes his temptations to sin, and learns to refine and redirect his desires in order to accomplish good things in the world, in the service of God.

Chapter 3

RELATING TO SUFFERING THAT OTHERS CAUSE TO ONESELF AND TO THE SUFFERING THAT OTHERS EXPERIENCE

Another test that can occur to a person is when someone else causes him to suffer, by cursing, hitting, abusing or degrading him, or similar bad conduct by which one person can inflict suffering upon another.[341]

The proper reaction of a pious person to abuse he receives from other people has been explained in the previous section (the Fifth Gate, Chapter 6). In this chapter, an expanded explanation will be brought.

Not only does a pious person not take revenge, but he should also recognize and consider the essence and condition of the person who caused him suffering. When someone is wronged with speech, it is possible that the other person was in a bad mood, and did not truly intend to harm, but was only speaking out of his own pain and suffering. Regarding such a case, King Solomon said, "A gentle reply turns away anger."[342] When a pious person focuses on the reality that the offender is surely suffering from problems of his own, he will actually set his heart to think about how he can help that person to have fewer troubles. This is the hallmark of a pious person: he aims to fix the wrong that was done and not leave it as an ongoing problem, and certainly not to make it worse, God forbid. But even if he did nothing and remained silent during and after the verbal abuse he received from the other person (and the best he could do was to keep the argument from getting worse), he still has to contemplate why God caused it to happen to him, and what the message is that God is giving him. In truth, this occurrence was prearranged by Divine Providence, and perhaps it was so that he could help or uplift the other person.

In some cases, the pious person will understand that the one who is wronging him with speech is just an evil person with a bad character,

---

[341] All that is mentioned in this chapter does not negate the need and permission for one to defend himself, his property, and his good name from others who would harm or oppress him. Here we discuss the understanding that everything comes from God; seemingly bad things are drawn down from a hidden level of Supernal Good, and may be a test or a message from God.

[342] Proverbs 15:1.

whose way of speaking to others is an expression of his meanness. Regarding such people, King Solomon said, "Do not answer a fool according to his foolishness, lest you be considered like him."[343]

This is specifically the situation in which a righteous person should remain silent and not answer back to the offender. This puts him on the level of pious people who accept to be among the pursued and not among those who pursue others, and among those who accept humiliation but not among those who humiliate others.[344] The main point, though, is that the person who is spoken against should not argue and fan the flames of the fight. Instead, he should take to heart that the occurrence came from God and try to perceive why.

A pious person should contemplate the fact that every "bad" occurrence also comes from God. It may be that on a revealed level it is connected with an apparently "random" course of events, such as sickness or the forces of nature. Or it may be that another person abused him, for God gives life to the abuser as well, and also directs the specific harm that he does. For even though the person who is causing the trouble has the freedom of choice to abuse or not (and he will therefore be punished by God for choosing to commit this sin, if he does not properly repent), nevertheless, it was already decreed by God that the victim would undergo this suffering.

When King David's son Abshalom attempted to overthrow him, and he had to escape from his capital Jerusalem, on the way he was cursed by Shimi, the son of Gaira. The following exchange then occurred:[345]

"Abishai the son of Zeruiah said to the king, 'Why should this dead dog curse my lord the king? I will go on ahead and take off his head!' But the king said, 'What does it matter to me or to you, sons of Zeruiah? He is cursing because God has said to him: Curse David. Who then shall [have the right to] say: Why have you done this? ... Let him be; let him curse, for God has told him to.' "

It is clear that God did not openly speak to Shimi and tell him to curse King David. Rather, the thought to do so arose in Shimi's mind

---

[343] Proverbs 26:4.

[344] Maimonides, *Laws of Personal Development* 5:13; Lamentations 3:30.

[345] II Samuel 16:9-11.

and heart, but it came from God, for with "the Breath of His Mouth" He gives life to the whole world and the particular details of everything in it, including the life-force of Shimi in particular at the time that he spoke these words to King David. If God would have chosen to taken away His Breath of Life from Shimi's power of speech, he would not have been able to say anything. Therefore, it is clear that God was giving him the ability to act on his desire to curse David at that time.[346] Hence, King David did not relate to the curse on a personal level, but that it was arranged by God with a purpose, as King David said. "Perhaps God will see [my suffering from this insult and the tears of] my eye, and God will return to me good instead of his [Shimi's] curse on this day."[347]

Thus is the way of those who are pious, to act kindly and to empathize with the pain and troubles of other people. Whoever sees a friend in pain and hides from him is a sinner, and certainly that is not the way of the pious.[348]

Nevertheless, one should learn from the lesson of Job's four friends, how not to speak to a person who is suffering, while he is being tested and his faith is being challenged. When they heard of his illness and tribulations, they all came with the initial good intention to comfort him and encourage him to the best of their abilities. (For when a person is beset with suffering, his friends feel pained by that as well and want to help.) But in the case of Job's friends,[349] three of them failed to do so, and instead spoke to him hurtfully and without wisdom – as it says, "They found no answer and condemned Job." The fourth spoke with wisdom, but he did so in anger and with his voice raised.

One must remember that the purpose of visiting people during their illness or distress is to show them support and pray for them, and beg God to grant them mercy. By visiting someone who is in distress, one can also best find out how to help fix the unfortunate situation, and to give gentle good advice for how the person can help himself with a wise plan of action or by improving his ways, or the like.

---

[346] *Igeres Hakodesh* (Tanya, Part IV), p. 276.

[347] II Sam. 16:12. Shimi later married and became the ancestor of Mordechai.

[348] See Tractate *Berachos* 12b.

[349] Job, ch. 32.

Chapter 4

THE TEST OF DEPRESSION[350]

The importance of serving God with joy was explained above in the Third Gate, Chapter 3, along with the importance of happiness in a person's life in general. Conversely, depression is a harsh and bad trait, which hinders a person's ability to serve God and have success in life, to the point that one can generally consider a fall into depression as a scheme of the evil inclination (as opposed to those for whom it is a chronic clinical medical condition, which is not discussed here).

Therefore, one must distance oneself from depression to the utmost, knowing that this is not the path of serving God. On the contrary, it makes one fall into the schemes of the evil inclination and give in to hedonistic pleasures of the physical world.

A person should contemplate and recognize the source of depression. If it comes from physical hardship, one should contemplate the matters elucidated earlier in this section, based on the verse,[351] "Happy is the man whom You chasten" – that one should be happy with the knowledge that everything comes from God and is for his ultimate benefit, although it is sometimes hidden from human comprehension. Through this one will believe and accept that this suffering comes from God for his good, which thereby eases the hardship, as explained earlier.

If the depression results from the hardship of one's spiritual standing (e.g., that the person is unable to overcome his evil inclination or the like), or that he had previously erred and done many sins, causing his heart to be broken, he should contemplate that the depression is only another scheme of the evil inclination. After it seduces a person to sin, it endeavors to cause him to completely give up hope in his effort to be righteous, so that through falling step by step, he will become subjugated to his sinful desires.[352] This is the way of warring nations: part of the battle is psychological warfare, in which one side tries to convince the other that it has no chance of winning, in order that its

---

[350] This chapter is based on *Likkutei Amarim* (Tanya, Part I), chs. 26 and 31.

[351] Psalms 94:12. Psalm 51 has a similar theme; see p. 188 in the Appendix.

[352] Or it may be from conceit, thinking he should already be completely righteous (a *tzaddik*), not needing to serve God by working at self-improvement.

forces will weaken and grow fearful, and be defeated more easily.

Regarding this tactic of the evil inclination, King David said: "I have become wise from my enemies"[353] – i.e., I will learn the ways and tactics of my enemies in order to be victorious over them.[354]

Since it is such a major goal of the evil inclination to draw a person into depression, one should understand from this that he has the power to overcome it, since God does not test a person with something he does not have the power to overcome. The first step to win the battle is the belief, happiness and trust that God always gives him the ability to act correctly.

One should contemplate that God, blessed be He, never despairs of him, and that God hopes he will return to Him in repentance and become a righteous person. This will bolster his understanding and faith that he has the power to be upright and fix his situation. With this he should be happy and trust in God, and get to work forthwith on bettering his ways in actual fact. **This is a powerful contemplation: Since God still has hope in me, surely I have true worth, and I am essential for the mission to do more good actions!**

The depression that comes from the evil inclination occurred with the first evil acts that were perpetrated by human beings in the world. It occurred to Cain, when he saw that his sacrifice to God was not accepted, despite the fact that his brother Abel's sacrifice was accepted. God counseled him not to give in to that test – as it is written:[355]

"And the Lord said to Cain: 'Why are you annoyed, and why has your countenance fallen?' [i.e.: Why are you falling into depression?] 'Is it not true that if you do well, you will be forgiven? But if you do not improve [yourself], at the entrance [of your grave], sin crouches; its longing is toward you;' [i.e.: The evil inclination desires to make you sin, and therefore it begins by seducing you to frustration. Then it continues to endeavor to subdue you with

---

[353] Psalms 119:98.

[354] This underscores that one should keep in mind that his evil inclination is his enemy and not his friend, and one should never be tricked to feel compassion or mercy for the unholy desires which God sends to test a person.

[355] Genesis 4:6-7.

depression that will cause you to despair. But if you sincerely try, although it is a challenge,] 'yet you can rule over it.' [i.e.: you, and not the evil inclination, are master over your body and your actions.]

This teaches that it is in your power to improve and not despair, but if you continue in the way of depression once it starts, you will fall prey to the plan of the evil inclination, which will continue to succeed in causing you to sin. (That is what actually did occur with Cain: he allowed his depression and jealousy to continue until it brought him to fall into the much greater sin of killing his brother Abel.)

However, there is a small advantage that one can draw out from a bout of depression if it happens due to one's hardship or lack of success in spiritual matters (described above) or material matters. The advantage is achieved by transferring the depression into a feeling of bitterness over the distance one has put between himself and God, by falling prey to mundane distractions which are akin to actual idolatry. This bitterness will cause one to abhor the triviality of one's mundane life, with its meaningless chasing after physical pleasures and honor.

This is *not* an end in itself. One must be careful that the temporary bitterness which is aroused will bring only a positive awakening, a renewed spirit and hopefulness in the heart (which is the opposite of depression, that instead results in despair, dullness and spiritual death). With this awakening, one can demand from himself that he abandon his pursuit of honor and worldly pleasures. Then the true positive purpose for this bitterness will be achieved, to motivate the person to take action and return to God. Then he should not retain it, God forbid, but rather replace it with the true joy that results from it, which is the joy of coming back under the "wings of the Divine Presence." (This is a phrase found in Ruth 2:12; see Rashi's explanation of Genesis 12:5.)

For the long term, one should regularly contemplate that to the extent which he desires and takes joy in the pleasures of the world, he will not have room in his heart for the higher pleasure of spiritual goodness. Then, when bitterness over one's fallen spiritual condition causes him to abhor worldly pleasures, his heart will break and thereby be cleansed from the follies of the world that he had attached to himself. With this, one's heart is opened and prepared to be happy with the truth of God, through one's faith and trust in Him, and in the results of the good actions that he can do.

The Seventh Gate:

The Gate of Repentance to God and the Principle of Reward and Punishment from God

Chapter 1

Contemplating Repentance to God

Every person is obligated to frequently recall and examine his actions, and make an honest accounting with his soul as to whether he has been acting in a correct and befitting manner in God's eyes. If a person finds that he has transgressed God's will in any of the universal Seven Commandments that he is obligated to fulfill, or that he has erred in his behavior or in any other matters which one is logically and morally bound to fulfill, he should sincerely regret this, and correct his path and behavior. He should accept upon himself that in the future, he will act only in an upright and correct manner, and not transgress any of God's Seven Commandments that He gave to mankind.

In this spirit, a penitent person is one who makes changes in his ways, to begin or return to serving God properly. In this process, he should sincerely ask God to forgive him for his past errors. This aspect of turning, or returning, to the path of righteousness in one's life is called *repentance*. In Hebrew, this is *teshuva*, which means *return* (to God).

A person should not imagine that his past actions are absolutely sealed before God, which would lead to the false conclusion that since he had sinned, it is impossible for him to now be a pious and upright person in God's eyes. That is not the truth, since God is merciful and gracious, and He waits for the repentance of sinners and their rectification of their sinful ways. When a sinner does repent correctly and abandons his bad ways, and accepts upon himself the yoke of God's Kingship (and to henceforth observe what God has commanded him to do and not to do), then God mercifully accepts him with open arms. God forgives him for the sins he has repented for, and does not punish him for those past errors that he regrets.

Solemn contemplation on the above great things that can be accomplished by repentance can bring a person to wholehearted love for God and yearning for His closeness.

God creates mankind and each individual. He also knows the characteristics of people in general, and the unique character of each and every person. Like everything in God's creation, it was His will to put the evil inclination into a person. Along with this, the ability to sin – either through temptation or carelessness – is fixed in a person's intellect, emotions and actions. Clearly, this is in a person's God-given nature. Therefore, God gives a person the ability and strength to correct and rectify himself through proper repentance, as recounted in numerous places throughout the Hebrew Bible about both Jews and Gentiles.

A person should not imagine that God is scheming against him. On the contrary, God loves every creation, and each being is created for His honor. If He did not desire us, He would not be continuously creating us. The good God, in His abundant love for mankind, wants each person to have what is best for him. Part of the good that God bestows upon a person is that he should be able to learn from experience, and sometimes the best way (or the only way) to learn is from one's own mistakes. Therefore, God in His great kindness gave people the path of repentance to rectify and improve themselves, and this is a true proof of His love for mankind.

The effectiveness of sincere repentance to God as an antidote for past sins can be seen in the case of the Gentile population of the Biblical city of Nineveh, as it says in the Book of Jonah:[356]

> And the word of God came to Jonah son of Amittai, saying, "Arise, go to Nineveh, the great city, and proclaim against it, for their wickedness has come before Me." ... Jonah began to enter into the city ... and he proclaimed and said, "In another forty days Nineveh will be overturned!" And the people of Nineveh believed in God ... it was proclaimed and declared throughout Nineveh by the counsel of the king and his nobles, saying: ... "Both man and animal shall cover themselves with sackcloth, and they shall call out mightily to God. Everyone shall repent of

---

[356] Jonah 1:1-2, 3:4-10.

his evil way and of the robbery that is in their hands." ...   And God saw their deeds, that they repented of their evil way; and God relented concerning the evil He had spoken to do to them, and He did not do it.

Likewise, when Cain was tempted to sin against his brother, God came to him and said to him, "הֲלוֹא (*Hallo! – Is it not so?*), if you will improve yourself, you will be forgiven ..."[357] As an eternal lesson for all generations, God instructed Cain about the ability to repent, which is in the hands of every person: to repent and return to God at any time one desires and makes the decision to do so, and God will forgive him.

---

[357] Genesis 4:7.

Chapter 2

Achieving a Complete Repentance[358]

A person has the ability to change for the better and repent for the duration of his life. This is an ongoing process, even step by step, and through this, God will forgive the person's sins. At the same time, it is important to know that there are many levels in the sincerity and truthfulness of a person's repentance, and in the degree to which his repentance under any given circumstances is accepted before God. Just as one who does a greater good deed will receive a greater reward than one who does a lesser good deed (as judged in God's eyes), so too, one whose repentance is greater and more completely truthful reaches a greater spiritual level in this respect than one who makes a repentance that is more limited, less complete or less truthful.

How could it be demonstrated that a person has a reached complete repentance for a sin that he committed? In one aspect, this is verified if he happens to find himself in the same type of situation in which he sinned before, and he is confronted with the option to do the sin again. Nevertheless, this time he refrains and does not commit the sin, only because he has decided to repent from that behavior, and not because of fear that people will see him, or lack of ability, etc.

For example, consider a man who engaged in sexual relations with another man's wife. After some length of time, they meet again in privacy, while their desire and physical ability still persist. But nevertheless, because the man resolved not to repeat his sin, he refrains and does not transgress. This demonstrates that his repentance was complete. Of course, this can apply to either the former adulterer or the adulteress. (Such a scenario is only relevant after it happened to take place. From the outset, a person is forbidden to deliberately put himself to a test. One should never be so sure of himself as to seek out tempting situations in order to be tested before God, especially since it may be that he was never before tempted with the full strength of his evil inclination. Since this was demonstrated by the case of the

---

[358] This chapter is mainly based on Maimonides, *Laws of Repentance*, ch. 2.

righteous King David in the incident with Bat Sheva,[359] how much more is it so for everyone else.)

On the other hand, if the adulterer does not regret his sin and repent until his old age, when he is impotent and incapable of doing the same sin that he did when he was younger, then this is not a high level of repentance. Nevertheless, God will still accept him as fully repentant. Even if a person transgressed throughout his entire life, and only repented on the day of his death and then died in repentance, the sins he repented for are forgiven by God.

In order to repent to God, a sinner should abandon his sins and strive to remove those inclinations from his thoughts, resolving in his heart never to commit them again – as it is stated, "May the wicked abandon his ways ..."[360] He must also regret his past sins – as it is stated, "After I returned, I regretted."[361]

What constitutes a prayer for forgiveness? The person should verbally confess his sins to God, and continue with stating the matters that he resolves in his heart about this. For example, one can say, "God, I have sinned before you by committing the sin of ... [explicitly stating the sin that was done]. Please, God, in your abundant mercy, pardon me for this sin. I am regretful and embarrassed for what I have done, and I have already resolved never to repeat it."

Anyone who verbalizes his confession without resolving in his heart to abandon the sin has not accomplished anything. In truth, by making an insincere confession, the person is making a mockery of himself before his Creator.

In some cases, for a person who repents for transgressions he committed publicly against other people, it is very praiseworthy to confess in public and to make his past sins known to others. He should tell them: "Although I sinned against so and so, committing the following misdeeds, ... now I am repenting and expressing my regret." Nevertheless, if one does not publicly confess a sin that he had done in public, but he does truly repent with all his heart and regrets his

---

[359] II Samuel, ch. 11.

[360] Isaiah 55:7.

[361] Jeremiah 31:18.

actions, this is also considered repentance (albeit an incomplete one), and he is forgiven by God.

For a sin done in private, however, it is not appropriate to publicize one's transgression, since doing so would be a disgrace to God's Name.

It is proper for the repentant person to cry out before God in supplication on a regular basis when he prays, and to give proper charity to the best of his capability. He should distance himself from the temptation or the situation of the sin he committed. He should strive to change his actions to be always good, and to walk in the correct path.

To repent for an extremely grave sin, such as murder, God forbid, the person should change his name, implying that he is no longer the same person as the one who did the sin, and he should exile himself to another place. It is taught in the Hebrew Bible that exile absolves one from sin, because it chastens a person and causes him to become humble and self-effacing.

Repenting only to God atones for sins between man and God; for example, idol worship, or eating meat that was severed from a living animal, or engaging in consensual forbidden sexual relations, or the like. However, sins against people – for example, injuring, cursing or robbing someone, or the like – will not be forgiven by God until the one who committed the sin makes restitution to the victim and asks for his forgiveness, and the victim is appeased and forgives him.

It is forbidden for a person who was wronged to be cruel and refuse to be appeased.[362] Rather, he should be easily pacified, and hard to anger. When the person who wronged him asks for forgiveness, he should forgive him with a complete heart and a willing spirit. After the sinner has appeased his colleague, he must then do correct repentance as outlined above, by regretting his sin, resolving not to repeat it, and confessing to God and asking Him for forgiveness.

It must be emphasized that even if a person makes restitution (for example, returning money that he wrongly took), he must also ask his victim for forgiveness and appease him. If a person wronged someone

---

[362] See Genesis 20:17 in regard to Abraham's righteous conduct of forgiving Abimelech, and Tractate *Bava Kama* 92.

who then died before restitution was made and forgiveness was asked, the wrongdoer should still repent to God and ask for His forgiveness. It is fitting that he should go to his victim's grave in the company of three other people, and ask for forgiveness from the victim's soul for the wrong that he did. If the wrong done was in money matters, he should return that amount to his victim's heirs. (If there are no heirs, he should disburse the money to proper charity, or consult a proper court or an expert rabbi about what he should do.)

A person should not think that repentance is only necessary for sins that involve speech or deeds, such as slander, idolatry, promiscuity, or theft. Rather, just as a person is obligated to repent from those types of sins, similarly, he must search out and strive to correct his bad character traits, whether he has them inherently or he learned them from others. He must turn away and repent from anger, hatred, envy, frivolity, greediness, honor-seeking, gluttony, and the like.

These bad character traits are more difficult to abandon and repent for than those that involve deeds. If a person is attached to any of these bad traits, it is more difficult for him to separate himself from them.[363] In this context it says, "May the wicked abandon *his* path, and the crooked man *his* designs, and he should return to God and He will have mercy on him, and to God, for His forgiveness is bountiful."[364]

---

[363] Maimonides, *Laws of Repentance*, ch. 7.
[364] Isaiah 55:7.

Chapter 3

How God Judges for Rewards and Punishments[365]

God judges all the speech and actions of a person, and thoughts can be included as well. This judgment is constant during one's life in the physical world, and when the physical lifetime ends, there is a summary judgment of the soul itself. At an eventual time in the future Messianic Era, the souls will be returned to their bodies for resurrection, to stand for their final judgment on the Judgment Day.

After one's passing, his soul is brought to the Heavenly Court in the spiritual realm, to be judged for each thing he did, and for the overall verdict on his entire life. All the person's thoughts, speech and actions are considered. God considers all the person's merits, but He only considers the sins that are unrepented. In His perfect judgment, God bestows reward for meritorious faith and good deeds, and decrees punishment for unrepented sins. This occurs both for the person during his physical life, and for his soul after he passes away. There are many levels of these rewards and punishments, both for the person in this world and for his soul in the next world.

Each and every person has merits and sins. A person whose merits exceed his unrepented sins in God's calculation is termed "righteous" *(tzadik)*, in the sense of being declared to be on the side of righteousness in God's overall judgment. A person whose unrepented sins exceed his merits in God's calculation is termed "sinful" *(rasha)*, in the sense of being declared to be on the side of sinfulness in God's overall judgment. If his merits and unrepented sins are judged to be equally balanced in God's calculation, he is termed "intermediate" *(beinoni)*.

This reckoning is not calculated only on the basis of the number of merits and sins, but also takes into account their magnitude in God's eyes, with all things being considered for that particular person. A person is likely to have some merits which for him will each outweigh many sins, as implied by the verse: "... because there is found in him a good deed toward the Lord, God of Israel."[366] In contrast, a person may have some sins which for him will each outweigh many merits –

---

[365] This chapter is mainly from Maimonides, *Laws of Repentance*, ch. 3.

[366] I Kings 14:13.

as it is stated, "One sin may obscure much good."[367] This relative weighing of sins and merits is unique for each person, and it is carried out according to the wisdom of the Omniscient God. Only God knows how to weigh the merits against the sins for each person.

The same applies to an entire country. If the total magnitude of the merits of all its citizens exceeds the total magnitude of their sins, it is termed "righteous" in God's judgment. If the total magnitude of their sins exceeds the total magnitude of their merits, it is termed "sinful." The same applies to the entire world.

If the sins committed by the people of a country are exceedingly numerous and extreme, God will bring it to oblivion, by destruction or by events that nullify their national identity. This is exemplified in God's statement to Abraham about the verdict He was placing upon the wicked people of Sodom and its surrounding metropolis: "And God said, 'Since the outcry of Sodom and Gomorrah has become great, and since their sin has become very grave; I will descend now and see, whether they have done according to the cry of it, which has come before Me – [I will bring] destruction, and if not, I will know."[368] This implies that God would examine the sins of each and every person, and that His righteous judgment would ensure that any righteous people in that population would be saved, even if they were only a small minority. God assured Abraham about this when He responded to Abraham's request and prayer that He consider any righteous people before His verdict for the population's destruction was sealed.[369]

In regard to the entire world as well, if the sins of humanity would become exceedingly greater than their merits, the wicked would be destroyed, as happened to the generation of the Flood.[370] The wicked

---

[367] Ecclesiastes 9:18.

[368] Genesis 18:20-21.

[369] Ibid., 18:25. This was borne out by the fact that God rescued Lot from the destruction of Sodom, and his family with him, on account of his merits, even though he was not entirely righteous.

[370] It would seem that citing the generation of the Flood is not relevant, because God swore in the Covenant of the Rainbow that He would never again bring a punishment of destruction upon the whole world. God's promise includes holding back from punishing by any worldwide destruction,

would perish, and the righteous would be saved, as were Noah and his family, as it is written, "God saw that the evil of mankind was great ... and God said: 'I will wash away man' ... But Noah found favor in the eyes of God."[371]

A person should always look at himself as equally balanced between his merits and sins, and the world as equally balanced between the total of its merits and the total of its sins. If he performs one sin, he may tip his balance and that of the entire world to the side of guilt and bring a verdict of punishment upon himself. On the other hand, if he observes one of his commandments or does a meritorious good deed, he may tip his balance and that of the entire world to the side of merit and bring deliverance and salvation to himself and to others. In this accounting, a person's observance of a prohibition can be greater in God's eyes than actively doing a good deed. As they relate to an individual, the Noahide Commandments themselves all involve prohibitions, and very often, refraining from a sin takes more effort in self-control and more submission to God's Kingship than doing a positive action.

A person who regrets good actions he has done and discredits his merits, saying in his heart, "What difference does it make that I have done them? I wish I had never done them," loses those merits, and does not receive a reward for any of them, as the verse says, "... The righteousness of the righteous will not save him on the day of his transgression ..."[372]

---

not only by a Flood. (See *Hisvaaduyos* 5745, 1st of Cheshvan, pp. 527-537; *Likkutei Sichot* v. 35, p. 31ff.) Also, humanity will never become that wicked again, and people have the ability to repent, which they did not have before the Flood. (See ibid. v. 15, p. 51ff; *Sefer HaSichot* 5751, p. 75ff.)

Nevertheless, Maimonides' points are correct in teaching that God judges on many levels: each individual, a community, a nation, and the whole world. Therefore, if the majority of the world everywhere were wicked, God would punish the world as a whole. (Even though there will never again be a punishment of worldwide destruction such as God brought through the Flood, there are other lesser types of punishment.)

[371] Genesis 6:5,7-8.

[372] Ezekiel 33:12. Although the simple words of the verse seem to say that a person will not be saved on account of his righteousness from punishment for

When God judges a person, the sins that were committed are weighed against the merits that were earned. For the determination of whether or not to bring a punishment, God does not consider a sin that was committed only once or twice; a sin is only considered to be punishable if it was committed three times or more. If the result is that even only those sins that were committed more than three times outweigh the person's merits, he is judged with all of his sins taken into account (even those that were committed only once or twice).

If his merits are equal to or greater than his sins that were committed three times or more, God forgives his sins one after the other, i.e., the third sin is forgiven because it is considered as a first sin, for the two previous sins were already forgiven. Similarly, after the third sin is forgiven, the fourth sin is considered as a "first" sin and is forgiven according to the same principle. The same pattern is continued until the consideration of all his sins is concluded.

When does the above apply? In the judging of an individual, as can be inferred from the verse, "All these things, God will do twice or three times with a man."[373] However, in regard to a community, punishment for the first, second, and third sins is withheld, as implied by the verse, "For three sins of Israel, I will withhold retribution, but for the fourth, I will not withhold it."[374] When God makes His reckoning of the community's merits and unrepented sins, it is made according to the above pattern, but the reckoning begins with the fourth sin.

This judgment of individuals, communities and nations occurs every year at the beginning of year in the Hebrew calendar, which is the day of Rosh Hashanah – the first day of the month of Tishrei, which falls in September or early October. That is also when God, the King of the universe, determines what the lot in life will be in the year ahead, for all people and all living creatures. God administers this judgment with mercy, for He allows a person's repentance, prayer and charity to avert

---

his sins, the sages explained in Tractate *Kiddushin* 40b that this verse refers to a righteous person who comes to regret his good deeds.

[373] Job 33:29.

[374] Amos 2:6.

the strictness of His decree, and those efforts by a person are especially effective in the 30 days before Rosh HaShanah. Even after Rosh HaShanah, a person can repent and be forgiven for the sins for which he was judged on Rosh HaShanah, and he can be shielded from punishment by doing more deeds of goodness, kindness and charity.

All of this applies while a person is still alive. When a person dies, there is no more opportunity for repentance, and his soul is given its summary judgment in the Heavenly Court. If in the balance of merits and unrepentant sins it is found to be righteous, it immediately merits to enter its place of spiritual paradise in the Heavenly firmaments, where righteous souls receive their reward for their service to God during their life on earth. If in the balance it is found to be sinful, it descends to *Gehinom*, which is the spiritual Purgatory. After the sinful soul is purged of its unrepented transgressions in *Gehinom*, it then ascends to its spiritual paradise to receive the reward for its merits.

It remains to explain God's judgment of a *beinoni* soul, at the intermediate level described above, whose unrepented sins are exactly balanced with its merits. If it does not have a sin of forbidden relations as part of its unrepented transgressions, then God, in His abundant kindness, turns the soul's balanced judgment to the side of righteousness and raises it to its spiritual paradise.[375] But if it has a sin

---

[375] Tractate *Rosh Hashanah* 17a. Maimonides, in *Laws of Repentance*, ch. 3, states that among Gentiles, only the pious have a share in the World to Come. It appears that he is including only those who observe all the Seven Noahide Laws as Divine commandments given by God through Moses at Mount Sinai, as he explains in *Laws of Kings* 8:11. In more detail, a Gentile who accepts the Torah's Seven Noahide Laws as his commandments, and accepts belief in the One God and the yoke of His Kingship, is guaranteed a share in the future World to Come, which will begin with the general resurrection of the righteous. If a person with this faith happens to infrequently transgress some of the Noahide Laws because of enticement from his evil inclination (and not on account of rejecting God's Kingship over him and/or the faith that the Noahide Laws are from God), he is still recognized by God as being a Pious Gentile. Thus, on the one hand, a person may be judged by God to be generally pious in regard to having the merit to receive a place in the future World to Come. But this does not change the fact that when he passes away, his soul is judged at that time according the principles described in this chap-

of forbidden relations as part of its unrepented transgressions,[376] God's judgment tips to the opposite side, and the soul is assigned to *Gehinom* because of its sins. After the soul is cleansed there, it then rises to receive its reward in its spiritual paradise.[377]

It is explained in the next chapter that this type of judgment and spiritual reward for the soul applies to a Gentile who accepts the details of the Noahide Commandments as being given from God, and that the spiritual reward for the soul of one who doesn't accept this is not eternal, and it is less in other respects as well.

There will also be a final judgment in the time of the future World to Come in the Messianic Era, at the time of the Resurrection of the Dead, as will be explained below in Chapter 8.

---

ter, as to whether, in the balance, he was righteous, intermediate or sinful (with only the unrepented sins being considered).

[376] Tractate *Rosh Hashanah*, ibid., regarding Noahides (unlike the ruling for the soul of a Jewish man who never fulfilled the Jewish commandment to put on phylacteries [in Hebrew, *tefillin*].)

[377] In this work, we do not discuss the subject of the possible reincarnation (in Hebrew, *gilgul*) of a soul. On that subject, see *Soul Searching*, by Yaakov Astor, pub. Targum Press, 2003.

Chapter 4

THE FUTURE WORLD TO COME AND WHO WILL MERIT THAT REWARD[378]

From prophets of the Hebrew Bible (Isaiah,[379] Ezekiel[380] and Daniel[381]) and sages of the Talmud,[382] it is known that in the Messianic Era, the world will reach the time of the Resurrection of the Dead, when God will bring back to life the righteous people of all the past generations, and openly reveal Himself to them. He will thenceforth dwell together with them, and that will be the eternal era of the World to Come, which will be the unique and wondrous ultimate spiritual reward. The meaning of "a portion in the World to Come" is the eternal cleaving of the person's body and soul with the Divine Presence, each person according to his own level and his own actions.

A Gentile merits to have a portion in that future World to Come if he accepts the Seven Noahide Laws and is careful to keep them, provided that he does this because God commanded them in the Torah and made it known through Moses that He had previously commanded the Children of Noah about them.[383] When a Gentile lives in this manner, he has ascended to the spiritual level of the "pious of the nations of the world" (i.e., a Pious Gentile).

Conversely, a Gentile who does not believe that these are commandments from God, nor that Gentiles are obligated in God's eyes to keep all seven of them, has no portion in that eternal World to Come in the future. Nevertheless, God will still reward him for his good deeds, either during his life in this physical world, or spiritually for his soul in its afterlife, or some combination of both. Either way, his reward for the more limited service he has done will be temporary (i.e., not

---

[378] This chapter is mainly from Maimonides, *Laws of Repentance*, ch. 3.
[379] Isaiah 26:19.
[380] Ezekiel 37:12-14.
[381] Daniel 12:2.
[382] See, for example, Tractate *Sanhedrin*, beginning of ch. 11.
[383] Maimonides, *Laws of Kings* 8:11.

eternal). Therefore, it has no comparison to the ultimate future reward in the World to Come.[384]

The following parable sheds light on these principles. A simple man who was riding on a horse once did a great favor for the king. The king decided to give him his deserved reward and made him one of the honorable officers of his court. For such a person, this is a complete change – he became a different person from his previous status as one of the simple townsfolk. The king also decided that the horse should receive its reward for serving its master and aiding him to do this great favor for the king (and also so the rider should not have to see his horse remain in the low state it was beforehand). The horse's reward was to live in a beautiful pasture with no work for the rest of its life. With this gift, it rested happily in a safe haven which was made specifically good for horses. So although the horse received a good and restful life, it remained a horse, and did not achieve any special greatness nor any change in its basic status.

In a similar way (although it is impossible to accurately describe or even comprehend), the reward that will be given by God in the World to Come for a Gentile who lived piously in His eyes will involve a great transformation. It will raise him to an immensely higher spiritual level that his soul previously could not attain, to perceive the Divine Presence and be filled with knowledge of God, while he continues living forever in his resurrected physical body.[385] By contrast, the reward for a Gentile who is not living piously in God's eyes is the type of physical or spiritual pleasures that he enjoys having in his life. Even after his death, God can give his soul spiritual pleasure until its due reward has been completely allotted.

There are also some people who are so bad that they have no portion in the future World to Come, and also no spiritual reward before that, in their afterlife. On account of their serious deliberate, rebellious, and unrepentant sins, the good deeds they did are not enough to tip their

---

[384] If one doesn't believe that these 7 commandments or the obligation to observe them are from God, he is not on the spiritual level of a Pious Gentile who does, and the reward for his soul in its afterlife does not compare at all to the greatness of the World to Come that is promised to a Pious Gentile.

[385] See *Sefer HaMaamarim 5628*, p. 40ff.

scale to the side of receiving any spiritual reward, even temporarily. Rather, their souls will be cut off forever from experiencing God's Presence. After their death, their souls are repaid in *Gehinom* for their unrepented sins and for remaining in their evil natures and attitudes throughout their lives.

(Although it was explained above in Chapter 3 that in general, souls receive some suffering in *Gehinom* for their unrepentant sins, the type of punishment that applies in this case – a person who conducted himself with extreme and unrepentant badness – is much greater. How so? In the first stage of the punishment, it is more severe: just as there are many levels for reward in the spiritual realms, so too, there are many levels of *Gehinom*, and these souls are taken to the most difficult level, until the time of the World to Come when *Gehinom* will cease to function. Then, in the second stage, they will be given complete *karet* (cutting off) from their source of existence, and they will cease to be. This can be illustrated with the following parable. A king punished two of his servants for their different offenses: the lesser offender was put into jail with small punishments for an allotted time, but he knew that he would return to the king's palace after he served his sentence. The second offender who committed a much more serious crime was not only banished from ever again being a servant of the king; he was placed in a dungeon with terrible suffering for many years, and then finally he was executed.)

This applies for Gentiles who remain unrepentant for the following serious transgressions: one who murders, one who habitually speaks evil gossip (*lashon hara* in Hebrew), one who sins unabashedly in public in order to desecrate God's Name, and one who commits apostasy. In this context, an apostate is one who makes a practice of willfully committing a particular sin, to the point that he gets so accustomed to committing it that he deems it to be permitted, and he acts as if there is no such commandment or prohibition against it from God.

It also applies to the following five categories of unrepentant people,[386] which will be explained below: (1) a "deviant believer" (a *min* in Hebrew); (2) a "scorner" (an *epicurus* in Hebrew); (3) a denier of the Torah;[387] (4) one who causes large numbers of people to sin; and (5) one who cruelly imposes fear upon large numbers of people.

1. Five types of people are in the category of a "deviant believer":

(a) one who maintains that there is no deity, and the world is not overseen;

(b) one who maintains that there are two or more gods that oversee;

(c) one who maintains that there is only one god, but having a body or form;

---

[386] The punishment for people in these five categories is the most severe, for the soul continues to suffer from fire taken from *Gehinom*, for a period of time after *Gehinom* ceases to function. See Tractate *Rosh HaShanah* 17a, which speaks about the extended punishment described in Isaiah 66:24.

[387] From *The Divine Code*, Part I, topic 1:12 and the footnotes there:

For a deviant believer, a scorner, or a denier of the Torah, this punishment does not apply if he has never known the truth because he has not learned about it. For such a person, it is incumbent upon one who does know God's truth to teach him that truth and the commandments that apply for him as a Gentile, and to correct and improve his ways. This is the proper guidance that Abraham provided.

For example, even though the Karaites deny the Oral Torah, in Maimonides' days they were not judged to be deniers, since for many generations they were raised from their birth in that culture, and compelled to follow that errant path.

Maimonides writes in *Laws of Kings* 10:1 that a Gentile is liable for transgressing a Noahide Commandment due to negligence, since he should have learned it. But it seems that he is only referring to a situation in which the general community knows the law, yet this person excluded himself and didn't learn it. If most of the members of the community don't know the law, one of these individuals is not liable unless he was previously warned, since it was impossible for him to learn it in his situation. Since the laws of God are true and just, such a person would not be liable under these unavoidable circumstances.

It is clear that this only applies to the Noahide commandments that need to be taught (since they are not dictated by logic), such as details of the prohibitions against worshipping idols.

(d) one who maintains that God was not the only First Existence and the Creator of everything, but rather there was a continuously existing primordial matter from which God formed the world;

(e) one who worships/serves an idol (or a star or constellation, or some other entity), having in mind that it will serve as an intermediary (a *shituf* in Hebrew) between him and God.[388]

2. Three types of people are in the category of a "scorner":

(a) one who maintains that there is no prophecy at all and no communication of knowledge from God to the hearts of individuals;

(b) one who denies the prophecy of Moses our teacher;

(c) one who maintains that God does not know the actions of people.

3. Three types of people are in the category of a "denier of the Torah":

(a) one who maintains that any of the commandments from the Torah scroll, or any of its text, are not from God (even if he nevertheless observes some or all of the commandments that are possible for him to observe, doing so because they seem to him to be logical or beneficial). This applies even if he holds that some of the commandments in the Torah came from Moses himself (from Moses' own intellect) instead of being from God;

(b) one who maintains that the Oral Torah and its explanations of the Torah's commandments originated not from God, but rather from Moses himself or from some other person(s). This applies even if he says that the Written Torah and its commandments were from God;

(c) one who maintains that God replaced any of the commandments He gave though Moses with another later commandment, or that His original Torah and commandments were later nullified. (This includes those who say that the "original" Torah which was given through Moses was true and from God, but it was later nullified, changed, or replaced).

---

[388] See *The Divine Code*, Part I (The Prohibition of Idol Worship), ch. 1.

4. The category of one who causes large numbers of people to sin includes:

(a) those who cause the people to commit a severe sin, like Jeroboam in the Book of I Kings, who caused the Ten Tribes to worship idols;

(b) those who cause the people to commit even a slight sin, even if it is only the nullification of a positive command.

These include both those who force the people to sin, and those who entice them to sin and lead them astray.

5. One who cruelly imposes fear upon large numbers of people is one who persecutes the community oppressively until they are very afraid of him, and he intends for this to enhance his own status, with no intention for increasing the honor of God. (This has often been the case for dictators or idol-worshipping kings, and it is similar to the category of those who bring large numbers of people to sin.)

God's judgment that a person in one of the above categories will not have a portion in the World to Come applies if the person dies without having repented. However, if such a person abandons his bad ways and dies in repentance (in Hebrew, *teshuvah*), he will merit to have a portion in the World to Come, for nothing can stand in the way of proper repentance. Even if he denied God's existence throughout his life and only repents and accepts God's Seven Noahide Commandments from the Torah in his final moments, he merits to receive a portion in the World to Come. (Therefore, it can be a great spiritual benefit to a Gentile who is nearing the end of his life, or even if he is on his death bed, if someone gently and sensitively informs him about the Seven Commandments for the Children of Noah that God included within the Five Books of Moses. Along with this, the person can be told about the benefit that will come to his soul if he will now accept these Divine commandments upon himself, and if he will also ask God to forgive him for having transgressed any of them during his lifetime.)

Chapter 5

Free Will[389]

Free will is granted to all people. If one desires to turn to the path of good and be righteous, the choice is his. Should he desire to turn to the path of iniquity, the choice is his. This is the intent of the Torah's statement: "Behold, man has become like the Unique One among us, knowing good and bad."[390] This teaches that humankind was made singular in the world, in that a person can, on his own initiative, objectively think about and know what is good and what is bad, and then choose to act according to his own will.

A person should not entertain the idea held by many fools, and what is claimed by some doctrines, that at the time of a person's conception or birth, the Holy One, blessed be He, decrees whether he will be righteous or a sinner. This is untrue. Each person is able to be righteous or bad. Similarly, he may be wise or foolish, merciful or cruel, miserly or generous, or he may acquire any other character traits. There is no one who compels him, sentences him, or leads him towards either of any two extremes. Rather, he tends to the character traits he chooses, based on his own initiative and decision.

This was implied by the prophet Jeremiah who stated: "From the command of the Most High, neither evil or good come forth [upon a person]."[391] This means that it is the sinner himself who causes his own loss. Nothing is gained if he deflects from his responsibility by looking for other excuses, as that leads a person to be content with merely complaining about his sins, instead of correcting them.

Therefore, it is proper for a person to cry and bemoan his sins and the damage he has done to his soul, and the negative consequences he brought upon it. This is implied by the following verse: "About what should a living man complain? A man *(gever)* for *his* sins"[392] – meaning, the sins which *he* owns. (There are several words in Hebrew which mean "man," and the world *gever* used here means a person

---

[389] This chapter is mainly from Maimonides, *Laws of Repentance*, ch. 5.

[390] Genesis 3:22.

[391] Lamentations 3:38.

[392] Ibid., 3:39.

with inner strength. This indicates that a person is endowed by God with enough strength to stop from sinning.) The prophet continues in the next verse to explain that since we have free choice, and it is our own decision that prompts us to commit a wrongdoing, therefore it is proper for us to repent and abandon our sins, for the choice to do so is present and in our hands: "Let us search and examine our ways and return to God."[393]

This principle is a fundamental concept and a pillar of the Torah and its *mitzvot*, as these verses state: "See, I have set before you today a blessing and a curse. The blessing that you will heed the command-ments of the Lord, your God, ... And the curse, if you will not heed the commandments of the Lord, your God,"[394] implying that the choice to do good or bad, according to your desire, is in your hands. The Creator does not compel or decree that people will do either good or bad. Rather, that is left to a person's own choice.

If God were to decree that an individual would be righteous or bad, or that there would be a quality that draws a person by his essential nature to any particular path of behavior, way of thinking, attributes, or deeds (which many of the fools believe are preordained by astrology), how could He command us through the words of His prophets such things as, "Do this," "Do not do this," "Improve your behavior," or "Do not follow after your own wickedness"? According to their mistaken conception, from the beginning of a person's creation, it would be decreed upon him, or his fixed nature would draw him, to a particular quality that he could not depart from. If this were so, what place would there be for the entire Torah? According to what judgment or sense of justice could retribution be administered to the wicked or reward bestowed the righteous? This was expressed by Abraham when he conversed with God: "It would be a sacrilege to You ... to put to death the righteous with the wicked, so the righteous should be like the wicked. It would be a sacrilege to You! Will the Judge of the entire earth not perform justice?"[395]

---

[393] Ibid., 3:40.

[394] Deuteronomy 11:26-28.

[395] Genesis 18:25.

A person should not wonder: "How is it possible for one to do whatever he wants and be responsible for his own deeds? Is it possible for anything to happen in this world without the permission and desire of its Creator?" Rather, one must know that everything is done in accord with God's will – as it is stated, "Whatever God wishes, He has done in the heavens and in the earth."[396] Nevertheless, we are responsible for our deeds.

How is this apparent logical contradiction resolved? Just as God established the nature of all the creations in the universe to be what He desired for them – for example, that in this world fire rises upward and water descends downward, and that the celestial bodies revolve in orbits – so too, He desired and established that people have free choice and responsibility for their good and bad deeds, without being forced, and whatever possible thing a person desires, he can choose to do. With this being the case, a person, on his own initiative, with the intellect that God has granted him, can choose between any of the things he is able to do within the circumstances that are being presented to him. Therefore, God judges according to the deeds a person does, while His judgment is tempered with His mercy in light of the true nature of the circumstances in which the deed is done. If the person acts correctly, God responds with beneficence. If he acts wrongly, there is a corresponding verdict. This is implied by these statements from the Prophets: "This [difficulty that will come upon you] is from your hand;"[397] and "They also have chosen their own paths."[398]

This concept was also implied by King Solomon in his statement, "Young man, rejoice in your youth ... but know that for all these things God will bring you to judgment;"[399] i.e., know that you have the potential now to do what you will, but in the future, you will have to account for your deeds.

---

[396] Psalms 135:6.
[397] Malachi 1:9.
[398] Isaiah 66:3.
[399] Ecclesiastes 11:9.

Chapter 6

THE OBSTRUCTION OF FREE CHOICE
AS A PUNISHMENT FROM GOD[400]

There are many verses in the Torah and the Books of the Prophets that appear at first glance to contradict the principle of free will for human beings, which is fundamental. Thus, many people err on account of those verses, and they think that a person's heart is not given over to him to direct it toward any path he desires. They also wrongly think that the Holy One, blessed be He, decrees upon a person to do good or commit evil. Therefore, it is important to explain a fundamental principle, on the basis of which the correct interpretation of those verses can be understood. This is the principle of how God may punish a person during his life in this world for freely choosing to commit bad actions.

When a person consciously and willfully transgresses against God's Law, it is proper for God to give a punishment, as explained. The Holy One, blessed be He, knows how to perfectly determine the correct and just punishment for an unrepented sin. The same applies to the people of a country who transgress collectively.

There are certain sins for which God's justice determines that punishment is to be administered in this world. This might be inflicted by God upon the sinner's body, or with trials and tribulations, or on his possessions, or on his small children. (God's punishment of a person may be administered through a Divine decree upon his small children who do not yet possess intellectual maturity, which applies for daughters under the age of 12, and sons under the age of 13. This concept is alluded to by the verse: "A *man* will die because of his own sins."[401] The wording of the verse means that it only applies after one has become an adult, because a Divine decree may come upon a young child as a punishment to the child's sinful parent.)

There are other sins for which God's justice determines that punishment is to be exacted upon a person's soul in its spiritual afterlife, with no damage coming upon the transgressor during his

---

[400] This chapter is mainly from Maimonides, *Laws of Repentance*, ch. 6.

[401] Deuteronomy 24:16; see Rashi's explanation there.

physical life in this world. There are other sins for which punishment is given both during the sinner's life in the physical world and in his afterlife.

The above applies only when the transgressor does not repent. However, if he repents, his repentance (*teshuvah* in Hebrew) is a shield against punishment. Just as a person can sin consciously and willfully, he also has the ability to repent consciously and willfully.

It may be that a person will commit such a great sin, or so many sins, without repenting, that God will then respond by not granting him an opportunity to repent from the bad ways that he has freely chosen to follow. Then, when the sinner eventually dies, his soul will be "cut off" because of the seriousness of the unrepentant sins that he committed against God. This is implied in the words of the Holy One, blessed be He, which were related by Isaiah: "Fatten the heart of this people, harden its ears, and seal its eyes, lest it see with its eyes, hear with its ears and understand with its heart, so that it will repent and be healed."[402] Similarly, it is stated, "But they mocked the messengers of God, scorned His words, and scoffed at His prophets, until the anger of the Lord mounted up against His people until there was no remedy."[403] This verse means that the people willingly sinned and multiplied their iniquity until it was determined by God to hold back their repentance, which is referred to as the "remedy."[404]

For these reasons it says in the Book of Exodus, "I [God] will harden Pharaoh's heart."[405] Pharaoh began to sin on his own initiative, as he

---

[402] Isaiah 6:10.

[403] II Chronicles 36:16.

[404] The meaning of this text is that although God usually assists a person and motivates him to repent, in these severe cases, God acts in an opposite matter as a punishment to this type of sinner, and sets up very difficult obstacles to the person's repentance so he will likely never repent.

Nevertheless, even for this level of sinner, God still leaves the person free choice to regret his ways so much that he can strengthen himself and seize the opportunity on his own to repent and be forgiven, even until his final moment of life.

[405] Exodus 14:4.

stated, "Come, let us deal cunningly with them [the Israelites]."[406] He then hardened his heart on his own initiative and decreed increasingly severe hardships upon the Israelites whom he had enslaved in his land. He then continued doing this even after he was warned by God through Moses, and after he and his nation were seriously harmed by several miraculous plagues. This continued until the point that measure for measure, God restrained Pharaoh from repenting by hardening his heart, to further increase the retribution upon him. The Holy One, blessed be He, informed Pharaoh about this, when He stated (through Moses), "On account of this I have left you standing, in order to show you My power ... And as for you and your servants, I know that you are not yet fearful of the Lord, God."[407] God did this in order to make known through Pharaoh to all the inhabitants of the world that when He withdraws His assistance for repentance, the sinner will continue with his evil without ever being able to repent, and as result he will die without having repented.

We find this in regard to Sichon, the evil Amorite king, as it is written, "...the Lord your God caused his spirit to be hardened and his heart to be obstinate ...,"[408] so that he and his sinful nation would wage war and they would be killed in battle.

Similarly, the Canaanite tribes were restrained from repenting because of their abominable acts of idolatry and sexual transgressions, so that they would wage war against the Israelites and be miraculously defeated – as the verse states, "For it was from God, to harden their hearts to battle against Israel ..."[409]

We also find that intervention by God against a person's repentance can be applied while He is giving a punishment for the sins. The Israelites in the days of Elijah were deeply involved in idol worship, and God punished them with a severe drought for an extended time while He held them back from repenting. When it came time for Elijah to call on God for His miracles to prove to them that their idols were false, he invoked God by declaring,[410] "Answer me, O Lord, answer

---

[406] Exodus 1:10.

[407] Exodus 9:16, 30.

[408] Deuteronomy 2:30.

[409] Joshua 11:20.

[410] I Kings 18:37.

me, and this people shall know that You are the Lord God, and You have turned their hearts backwards" (i.e., away from repenting).

In conclusion, the Almighty did not decree that Pharaoh would oppress the Israelites, or that the Canaanites would perform abominable sexual acts and idolatry, or that the Israelites would worship idols. They all repeatedly committed great sins in open defiance of God on their own initiative, until God finally responded by restraining their repentance when it came time for Him to judge and punish them.

This is what is implied by the requests of the prophets and other righteous people in their prayers that are recorded in the Hebrew Bible, asking God to help them go in the path of truth. It was in this spirit that King David pleaded, "God, show me Your way that I may walk in Your truth;" [411] i.e., do not let my sins prevent me from reaching the path of Truth which will lead me to appreciate Your way and the Oneness of Your Name. A similar intent is conveyed by King David's request: "support me with a generous spirit." [412] By these words, he had this intention in his prayer: "Let my spirit be willing to do Your will, and do not cause my sin to prevent me from repenting. Rather, let the free choice remain in my hand until I repent, and comprehend and appreciate the path of Your Truth." All the verses in the Hebrew Bible which resemble these have a similar interpretation.

Likewise, we find David's statement: "God is good and upright, therefore, He instructs sinners in the path. He guides the humble in the path of justice and teaches the humble His way." [413] This means that God shows people the path of Truth, to encourage them to repent to Him. (This is seen many times in the Hebrew Bible, when God sent His prophets to inform people of the correct path, and how to be righteous and repentant). It was for that purpose that the words of Moses, the greatest of the Hebrew prophets, were recorded for the posterity of all mankind. Furthermore, it implies that God grants people the ability to learn and understand what He expects from them. This ability is present in everyone who is intellectually and mentally sound, so that as long as a person follows the ways of the wisdom and

---

[411] Psalms 86:11.

[412] Psalms 51:14.

[413] Psalms 25:8-9.

righteousness that are set out in the Hebrew Bible, he will desire them and pursue them. This may be inferred from the statement of the sages of blessed memory: "One who comes to purify himself is assisted [by God];"[414] i.e., he finds that God is helping him in his effort to purify his ways.

---

[414] Tractate *Yoma* 38b.

Chapter 7

THE HEAVENLY REWARD FOR A DEPARTED SOUL; A PERSON'S REWARD IN THE FUTURE WORLD TO COME[415]

There are two eras that are available in the afterlife for people's souls. The first era occurs after one's life in the physical world, when one's soul ascends to its spiritual paradise in the heavenly realms. (If it merits, this may happen immediately after the person dies, or if not, it may happen after a period of suffering in *Gehinom*, which brings about the purification of the soul from its unrepented sins.) In the spiritual paradise, there is no body or physical form. There is only the souls of the righteous alone, without a body, similar to the ministering angels. Since there is no physical form, there is neither eating, drinking, nor any of the other bodily functions of the physical world.

Do not think lightly of this good, by imagining that the heavenly reward for a person's observing his commandments and following the paths of God's Truth is for him to eat and drink good foods, have intercourse with beautiful forms, wear garments of linen and lace, dwell in ivory palaces, use utensils of gold and silver, or other similar ideas, as conceived by those who are foolish.

In contrast, true sages and people with correct knowledge know that all such conceptions of the afterlife are vain and empty things which do not lead one to the path of properly serving God. These physical things are considered to be desirable or beneficial to us in this world because we possess a body and a physical form. The natural soul desires them and lusts for them for the sake of the pleasures and honor of the body, so that its desires will be fulfilled and its health maintained. A wise person knows that God presents the needs of the body to us so we can choose to use them for aiding us to serve Him in this world. In the afterlife, when there is no body, all of these matters are nullified, and the soul forgets about them.

Beyond this, the ultimate good that is stored away for the righteous is the life of the future World to Come, which will be revealed in the second stage of Messianic Era. When that time begins, the souls will return to their bodies with the Resurrection of the Dead, as will be

---

[415] This chapter is mainly from Maimonides, *Laws of Repentance*, ch. 8.

explained in the next chapter. This will be a perfected life that is not accompanied by death, and a higher level of good that is not accompanied by evil. The Torah alludes to this in the promise: "... so that it will be good for you, and you will prolong your days."[416] The Oral Tradition explains:[417]

"... so that it will be good for you" – in the world that is entirely good; "and you will prolong your days" – in the world that is endlessly long, the World to Come.

The main reward of the righteous is that they will merit this spiritual pleasure and take part in this eternal good.

The retribution for the wicked is that they will not merit this eternal life of pure good and revealed Godliness. Rather, their souls will eventually be cut off from their source of spiritual life from God, and thus automatically die, in a similar fashion as the beasts that have no afterlife. This is the meaning of the Divine punishment known as *karet* ("cut off") for specific severe sins within God's Law, which appears many times in the Torah with the statement: "that soul shall 'surely be cut off' *(hikaret tikaret)*."[418] Regarding the repetition of the verb in that verse, the Oral Tradition explains:[419] *hikaret* means to be cut off in this world, and *tikaret* means to be cut off in the World to Come. After the souls that are judged to receive *karet* become separated from their bodies in this world, they will not merit to have the resurrected life of the World to Come. Rather, even in the World to Come, they will be cut off. For Gentiles, the sins that incur *karet* are unrepented deliberate transgression of any of the specific Seven Noahide Commandments, or willful rejection of the fundamentals of acceptance[420] of the One God and the Torah of Moses, or bringing sin or fear upon large numbers of people.

---

[416] Deuteronomy 22:7.

[417] Tractate *Kiddushin* 39b.

[418] For example, in Numbers 15:31.

[419] *Sifri* (on Numbers) 112, p. 121.

[420] The categories of this rejection are the "deviant believers," "scorners," and "deniers of Torah" that are described above in this section, in Chapter 4.

It is written in the Talmud, "In the World to Come, there is neither eating, drinking, nor sexual relations. Rather, the righteous will sit with their crowns on their heads and delight in the radiance of the Divine Presence."[421] Maimonides gave the following explanation:[422]

"... the phrase, 'their crowns on their heads,' is [a metaphor, implying] that they will know the [inner meanings of the Torah] knowledge that they grasped [during their lives] ... This will be their crown. [Further support that the 'crowns' will not be physical[423] is found in the prophecy:] 'Eternal joy will be upon their heads.'[424] Joy is not a physical entity that can rest on a head. Similarly, the expression 'crown' used [there] by the sages refers to knowledge [which is a spiritual concept]. What is meant by the expression, 'delight in the radiance of the Divine Presence'? They will know and grasp the [hidden] truths of Godliness ..."

---

[421] Tractate *Berachot* 17a, in the name of the sage Rav.

[422] *Mishneh Torah, Laws of Repentance* 8:2.

[423] The future World to Come has never been seen except by God Himself, as Isaiah declared (64:3), "No eye has seen it but Yours, oh God." Its actual state of being was therefore left open to differences of opinion. By explaining the words of the Talmud in a completely spiritual context, Maimonides was bringing support for his opinion that the ultimate World to Come will be entirely spiritual, and that the righteous who merit it will exist there only as purified souls with no physical bodies, after a temporary period of physical resurrection. However, other *Rishonim* sages – including Nachmanides (see *Sha'ar HaGmul*) and Ra'avad (see his commentary on *Mishneh Torah*, ibid.) – as well as the Chassidic masters, strongly disagreed and maintained that in the ultimate World to Come, the Essence of God will be revealed eternally to the righteous while they exist as souls living in their resurrected physical bodies, in the physical world.

Although Maimonides was probably writing specifically about the spiritual revelations that the Jews will have in the future World to Come (at which time they will all truly serve as the "light to the nations"), we can appreciate that the eternal reward of the Pious Gentiles will be somewhat in a parallel path of progress – an elevation of their souls and their spiritual awareness to the highest of levels in the spiritual worlds. For the Chassidic view on these matters, see for example *Sefer HaMaamarim 5628*, in the discourses starting on p. 40 and p. 42.

[424] Isaiah 51:11.

There is no way in this world to accurately grasp and comprehend the ultimate good that the soul will experience in the World to Come. We only know the good we can experience now, and that is what we desire. In contrast, the future ultimate good is overwhelmingly great and cannot be compared to the good of this world, except in a metaphoric sense.

Nevertheless, this concept can be somewhat understood through the parable of the various types of pleasures that a person can receive in the present physical world. One can receive *physical* pleasure on a base level from eating tasty food, and on a more refined level from hearing good music. One can receive *intellectual* pleasure from understanding a deep insight. A *soulful* pleasure can be experienced from doing a favor for another person, and seeing that person receive pleasure from the favor. Many other things in this world can give a person various levels of pleasure. Those pleasures that are felt by a person's senses, such as the taste of food, cannot reach the level of pleasure that one can receive from the higher human faculties, such as comprehension and happiness. The more refined the faculty, the greater and more uplifted is the pleasure it can receive.

For an intellectual person, the pleasure in the comprehension of a new concept is much more desirable than the physical pleasure of good tasting food. To such a person, the taste of food is comparable to an animalistic pleasure, since animals also eat and enjoy their food.

By contrast, one who has a very low level of intellectual capacity will take very minimal pleasure in understanding a new concept. He takes more pleasure in eating good food. But to a person with a spiritually refined intellect, that would be considered a minimal and insignificant level of pleasure.

In a similar vein, one can understand that all the pleasures of this world are like nothing in comparison to the transcendent spiritual pleasures that will be experienced in the World to Come.

In truth, there is no way to compare the good of the soul in the World to Come with the bodily pleasures of this world. Rather, that future good is immeasurably greater, with no comparison or likeness to anything else. This is alluded to by David's statement: "How great is the good that You have hidden for those who fear You."[425]

---

[425] Psalms 31:20.

But if the souls of the righteous must be returned to resurrected physical bodies in order to experience their ultimate reward, how does it differ from what the body can experience now in the present physical world? When God will resurrect the bodies of the righteous, He will not restore them to the way they were before, in the world as we know it. Instead, He will recreate them in a spiritually refined and immortal condition, in which one's very flesh will experience a unity with God.

How very much did David desire the life of the World to Come, as implied by the verse: "Had I not believed that I would see the goodness of God in the land of the living!"[426] This was also implied by Isaiah's statement: "No eye has ever seen, O God, except for You, what You will do for those who wait for You."[427] By this he meant that the future good, which was stored away by God for those who serve and wait for Him, has never been able to be perceived by the vision of any prophet, because it is too exalted to be perceived by any created being in the present world.

---

[426] Psalms 27:13. Rashi explains: "I know that You give reward to the righteous in the World to Come, but I do not know whether I have a share with them or not."

[427] Isaiah 64:3.

Chapter 8

THE MESSIANIC ERA AND THE RESURRECTION OF THE DEAD

The Oral Torah teaches that God created seven things before He created the world: Torah, Repentance, *Gan Eden* (the spiritual Garden of Eden), *Gehinom* (the spiritual Purgatory), His Throne of Glory, the Holy Temple, and the name of the Messiah.[428] This means that it arose in God's thought that these things were necessary for the existence of the world that He would create.[429]

God, blessed be He, created His world for the purpose He desired – as the sages said, "God desired to have a dwelling place in the lowest [i.e. physical] world."[430] This clearly teaches that God's objective for His creation of the world was to make a physical place which would be perfectly fitting for His Presence to rest in. The service of all mankind beginning from the time of Adam, the first person, is to contribute to reaching this objective. God has promised through His prophets in the Hebrew Bible that His desired future time will be realized through the coming of the true Messiah, from the dynasty of King David, who will usher in the era when all people will see God's truth and the righteousness of all His ways – as the verse says, "And the glory of God will be revealed, and all flesh will see together that the mouth of God has spoken."[431]

Therefore, from before the beginning of time, when God thought to create the world, He also thought of the intended purpose of the world. The seven things listed above are the goals of the creation of the world.

Torah: The Hebrew word *Torah* means "instruction." This is the revelation of God's will and His ways to human beings, teaching the way by which they can make the world into a place that is worthy for His Essence to be dwelling in, openly and permanently.

Repentance: This word in Hebrew is *teshuvah*, which literally means "return." It is the process by which a person recognizes his true

---

[428] Tractates *Pesachim* 54a, *Nedarim* 39b.

[429] Ran on *Nedarim, ibid.*

[430] Midrash *Numbers Rabbah* 13:6.

[431] Isaiah 40:5.

spiritual standing – how he has distanced himself from God – and he is therefore motivated to correct himself and his ways to thereby restore the bond of his soul with his Creator – as the verse implies: "And the spirit will return to God Who gave it [within a person]."[432] This means that a person's spirit [his soul] will return to its connection with God, its Creator, to achieve the closest bond it can have with the Divine Presence while living within this world. About this process of personal repentance, the prophet said,[433] "Let the wicked abandon *his* way, and the man of iniquity *his* thoughts; let him return to God, and He will have compassion upon him; and [let him return] to our God, for He will abundantly pardon."[434] *Teshuvah* in its essence – coming personally closer to God – applies at all times, and even to a person who has never sinned.

Gehinom and **Gan Eden**: These are the spiritual Purgatory and the highest spiritual Paradise, respectively, and both of them have numerous levels. These are where a departed soul[435] may receive its due punishment and cleansing from unrepented sins, or its due spiritual reward, after being judged by God.

At a time in the future, *Gehinom* will end and the souls in *Gan Eden* will return to physical bodies in the World to Come.

The Throne of Glory: This is the spiritual manifestation of God's Kingship over the creation. By making this known and famous worldwide through the visions He granted to His Biblical prophets, God rightfully demands that in every generation, mankind in general – and every individual – must recognize His omniscient Kingship, and accept the yoke of His commandments that He gave in His Torah (those for Jews and those for Gentiles).

The Holy Temple: This is God's House – His chosen place for the most open revelation of His Divine Presence in the world. The spiritual bond of the creation and its Creator is consummated through the service in the Holy Temple, which He commanded in Leviticus.

---

[432] Ecclesiastes 12:7.

[433] Isaiah 55:7.

[434] See Maimonides, *Laws of Repentance*, ch. 7, and *The Divine Code*, Part I (Fundamentals of the Faith), ch. 9.

[435] *Yalkut Shimoni, Yechezkel*, lists nine people who entered *Gan Eden* alive.

The name of the Messiah: The true Messiah (*Moshiach* in Hebrew) will be Jewish by natural birth and a direct patrilineal descendant of King David's son Solomon. He will be chosen by God to teach all people to fulfill God's will, and to rectify the world so that mankind as a whole will serve only God – as it is written, "And God shall become King over all the earth; on that day shall God be One, and His Name One."[436] *Moshiach* will complete the purpose of creation – the process which was begun by the righteous Patriarchs, Abraham, Isaac and Jacob – to spread the knowledge of the Oneness of God to all people throughout the world.

The promise of the arrival of *Moshiach* in the "End of Days" (which we have reached at this point in history) is written expressly in Torah. In the End of Days, the Jewish people will repent and be redeemed by God from their exile – as it is stated:[437]

"And it shall be when all these things have come upon you [the Jewish people] – the blessing and the curse which I have set before you – then you will take it to your heart among all the nations where the Lord your God has dispersed you; and you will return unto the Lord your God, and listen to His voice, according to all that I [Moses] command you this day – you and your children, with all your heart, and with all your soul. Then the Lord your God will bring back your captivity and have mercy upon you, and He will gather you in from all the peoples to which the Lord your God has scattered you. If any of you that are dispersed will be in the ends of the heavens [i.e., very distanced spiritually from God], from there the Lord your God will gather you in, and from there will He take you. And the Lord your God will bring you into the Land [of Israel] which your forefathers possessed, and you shall possess it; and He will make you better and make you more numerous than your forefathers. And the Lord your God will circumcise your heart and the heart of your children, to love the Lord your God with all your heart and with all your soul, that you may live."[438]

---

[436] Zechariah 14:9.

[437] Deuteronomy 30:1-6.

[438] See Maimonides, *Laws of Repentance*, ch. 7.

It is stated in other places in Torah that this redemption will be accomplished through the Messiah,[439] as explained by Maimonides in *Laws of Kings*, Chapter 11. In the Books of the Prophets, these matters are further explained at great length and in great detail.

This rectification of the Jewish people, which is prophesied in the Torah, will bring the rectification of all mankind, since the revelation of God's Divine Presence (the *Shechinah*) will return to the world and dwell most openly in the Third Holy Temple, which *Moshiach* will build in Jerusalem. This will be the revelation of God's Presence as it was in the beginning of the world, in the physical Garden of Eden. But it will be in an even greater way than ever before, with a Divine light that will illuminate and spiritually uplift the entire world. Emanating from the Holy Temple and the Jewish people, this Divine light will spread throughout the world to rectify everything and motivate everyone to serve only the One God.[440]

In that era, the character of mankind will be changed to recognize the spiritual truth and to desire only God. Each person will leave his previous faulty ways – as the prophet says, "For then I will turn the peoples to a clear language [i.e., a clear conception of truth and God-liness], so that all will call upon the Name of God to serve Him as one shoulder [i.e., "shoulder-to-shoulder," all together as one people]."[441]

In that era, there will be neither famine nor war, envy or competition, for good will flow in abundance, and all the good delights will be freely available as dust. The occupation of the entire world will be solely to know God – as the verse states:[442] "The world will be filled with the knowledge of God as the waters cover the ocean bed."[443]

After that era of the Days of *Moshiach*, there will be an incomparably more wondrous period – the eternal era of the Resurrection of the Dead – which is called the "World to Come." It will be the time of

---

[439] See Numbers 24:17-18, where Bilaam prophesied about King David in the future, and the King *Moshiach* in the far future.

[440] See Isaiah, ch. 60.

[441] Zephaniah 3:9.

[442] Isaiah 11:9.

[443] Maimonides, *Laws of Kings* 12:5.

the full Divine revelation and the ultimate spiritual reward that God is holding in store for the righteous.

What will be the distinction between the era of the Days of *Moshiach* and the era of the World to Come? In the Days of *Moshiach*, the world in general will still be in its natural condition. People will continue to eat, drink, sleep, and be occupied with all the body's physical needs, while at the same time, a person will be able to connect his mind and emotions with expanded knowledge of God, blessed be He. Therefore, there will also be birth and death in that era, although the natural human lifespan will be greatly increased.[444]

In the subsequent era of the World to Come, the natural order will be removed. The physical existence of every creation will be unnoticeable in comparison to its Godly essence that will be openly revealed, like a tiny flame of a match when it is held up before the face of the sun. There will be no physical bodily needs, and yet the body will continue to exist, recognizing and unifying with God according to a greatly increased and indescribable capacity. There will no more eating, drinking, sleeping, birth or death. Regarding this time, the verse states: "Death will be swallowed up forever ..."[445]

All the righteous from all past generations who will merit to live in that era will be resurrected and will come back to life, with their souls in their spiritually perfected bodies and their minds complete with the knowledge of God. They will derive boundless pleasure from the openly revealed shine of the Divine Presence, each one according to his capability as accomplished through his former observance of God's commandments and his deeds of goodness and kindness, by which he gained eternal merit.

At the beginning of the era of the Resurrection of the Dead, there will be the Day of the Great Judgment, which is referred to in the Books of the Prophets and the teachings of the sages in the Oral Torah. The various eras of the time of the Messianic Redemption – the time of the Resurrection, the time of the Judgment Day, and era of the World to Come – are all stated in the Book of Daniel: "And at that time [the

---

[444] See Isaiah 65:20, "... the youth who is one hundred years old shall die ...;" i.e., a person who dies at the age of 100 will have died in his youth.
[445] Isaiah 25:8.

archangel] Michael will stand up, the great prince who stands for the children of your people [Israel], and there shall be a time of trouble such as never was, from the time there became a nation [of the Biblical people of Israel] even to that time. And at that time, your people shall be delivered, every one that shall be found written in the Book. And many of them that sleep in the dust of the earth shall awake ..."[446]

On that Day of Great Judgment, all people of all generations will be judged for their actions. Although people are judged during their lifetime every year on Rosh HaShanah, and again when their soul departs, there will yet be a day of Great Judgment for all the actions of all people who ever lived.

In that judgment there will be three categories: the righteous, the intermediates, and the wicked. The righteous will merit the World to Come in the most complete fashion, where each one will receive a level of revelation of Godliness that corresponds to that person's own spiritual level and merits. The intermediates and the wicked will be judged for their actions, and the judgment for the intermediates will be more lenient than that of the wicked. Nevertheless – with some specific exceptions among the wicked as explained below – they will all merit the World to Come after they are sentenced to a painful purging of their sins to thereby become refined. Then they too will merit to receive a measure of Divine light as their reward for the good actions they did,[447] for they believed in the One God, yet they transgressed willfully or mistakenly due to the seduction of their evil inclination.

However, the exceptions are the people among the wicked who were "those that have rebelled against Me" – the *minim* and apostates who did not believe in the One God and His Torah, and the others mentioned in Chapter 4 who have no part in the World to Come, who knowingly rebelled against the existence of God and His commands. Instead, they are judged for their rebellious wickedness and sins that

---

[446] Daniel 12:1-2.

[447] This is the explanation in Tractate *Rosh Hashanah* 16b: "There will be three categories on the Day of Judgment ...," etc., based on Rashi and Tosafos there, and Nachmanides in *Sha'ar HaGmul* and other *Rishonim* sages.

condemn them for all eternity.[448] Regarding these people, the sages of the Talmud[449] cited the following verses in the Hebrew Bible.

The Book of Isaiah concludes with the words, "And they shall go forth and look upon the carcasses of the people who rebelled against Me; for their worm shall not die, nor shall their fire be quenched; and they shall be an abhorrence unto all flesh."[450] Near the conclusion of the Book of Malachi it is stated, "For behold, the day is coming, burning like an oven, when all the wicked people and the evildoers will be like straw; and that coming day will burn them up, says God, Master of Legions, so that it will not leave them a root or branch"[451] (i.e., they will cease to exist forever, without having had any standing or deliverance). And in the final chapter of the Book of Daniel it says, "Many of those who sleep in the dusty earth will awaken; these [the righteous] for everlasting life, and these [the wicked] for shame, for everlasting abhorrence."[452]

The righteous who merit the World to Come will take pleasure in the revealed Divine Presence, and they will shine with the great spiritual light that will glow from the good actions they did in their lifetimes – as it says: "The wise [who followed the One God] will shine like the radiance of the firmament, and those who teach righteousness to the multitudes [will shine] like the stars, forever and ever."[453] They will be spiritually uplifted from the concealments of bodily life, as explained above, yet will still remain with a connection to their bodies (similar to Moses when he ascended to Heaven to learn Torah from God for forty days without eating bread or drinking water; his body was sustained directly from the Godly spirit that is its true existence, without the

---

[448] Maimonides, *Laws of Repentance* 3:6-13. (Maimonides also lists some additional categories that apply only to Jews.) After these Gentile souls cease to exist, they will not be brought back.

[449] Tractates *Rosh Hashanah* 17a, and *Avodah Zarah* 4a.

[450] Isaiah 66:24. Their fire will continue for a time after *Gehinom* ends.

[451] Malachi 3:19.

[452] Daniel 12:2. Their shame is that they did not earn any level of the World to Come, and there will be an everlasting abhorrence of the evil ways that they followed, which will continue to be remembered by the righteous.

[453] Ibid. 12:3.

intermediary of physical worldly sustenance). They will see the revealed Truth of God and the great kindness in all His ways.

It appears from the Books of the Prophets that after the Day of Great Judgment, all people will regularly come to bow down and pray in the eternal Third Holy Temple in Jerusalem, which is the central place of prayer for all time and for all people, and from there the glory of the revealed Divine Presence will shine forth to the entire world – as it is written, "And it shall be that on every New Moon and on every Sabbath, all people [at that time] will come to prostrate themselves before Me [at the Third Temple], says the Lord."[454]

---

[454] Isaiah 66:23.

APPENDIX

Some Recommended Prayers for Noahides

❧ Daytime Prayers ❧

Upon awakening, a person should consider in Whose Presence he lies; he should be mindful of the Supreme King of kings, the Holy One, blessed be He, as it is said (Isaiah 6:3), "The whole world is filled with His glory."

After preparing oneself for prayer, recite these two paragraphs:[455]

I offer thanks to You, living and eternal King, for You have mercifully restored my soul within me; Your faithfulness is great.

Lord of the universe, Who reigned before anything was created – at the time when His will brought all things into being, then was His Name proclaimed King. And after all things will be uplifted, the Awesome One will reign alone. He was, He is, and He shall be in glory. He is One, and there is no other to compare to Him, to call His equal. Without beginning, without end, power and dominion belong to Him. He is my God and my ever-living Redeemer, the strength of my lot in time of distress. He is my banner and my refuge, my portion on the day I call. Into His hand I entrust my spirit when I sleep and when I wake. And with my soul, my body too, the Lord is with me, I shall not fear.

Psalms of praise: *Recite* Psalm 145; *one may add* 146, 150 *or others.*

Recite the following before accepting God's Unity and Kingship (see fn. 80):

Our Father, merciful Father Who is compassionate, have mercy on us, and grant our heart understanding to comprehend and to discern, to perceive, to learn and to teach, to observe, to practice and to fulfill Your will with love. Enlighten our eyes in Your wisdom, cause our hearts to cleave to Your Seven Commandments, and unite our hearts to love and fear Your Name, and may we never be put to shame, disgrace or stumbling. Because we trust in Your holy, great and awesome Name, may we rejoice and exult in Your salvation. Lord our God, may Your mercy and Your abounding kindness never, never forsake us.

---

[455] From the traditional *Siddur* prayer book liturgy.

Recitation to verbally accept God's Unity and Kingship:[456]

Almighty God, we accept upon ourselves that which is written in Your Torah: "You shall know this day and take to your heart that God [alone] is God, in the heavens above and on the earth below – there is none other!"[457] We affirm the precepts of "You shall love God, your God, with all your heart, and all your soul, and all your might;"[458] and "Fear God, your God, and serve Him, and in His Name [alone] shall you vow;"[459] and, as it says, "Fear God and keep His commandments, for that is a person's entire duty."[460]

For devout prayer, asking God for one's needs:

Blessed are You, God, the Supreme Being who bestows abundant kindness.

Please endow us graciously with wisdom, understanding and knowledge.

Please accept our repentance, and forgive us for our errors and sins.

Grant complete healing for all our wounds and ailments.

Bestow upon us all the needs for our sustenance from Your bounty.

Hasten the day of which it is said: "God will be King over the entire earth; in that day God will be One and His Name One;"[461] "For then I will turn the peoples to pure language, so that all will call upon the Name of God to serve Him with one purpose;"[462] and "They will not harm or destroy on all My holy mountain, for the earth will be filled with knowledge of God as water covering the sea bed."[463]

Hear our voice, God, our merciful Father, have compassion upon us and accept our prayers in mercy and favor. Blessed are You, God, who hears prayer.

---

[456] The prayers on this page, and the following *Prayer of the Repentant*, were authored by Rabbi J. Immanuel Schochet, o.b.m.

[457] Deuteronomy 4:39.

[458] Ibid. 6:5.

[459] Ibid. 6:13.

[460] Ecclesiastes 12:13.

[461] Zechariah 14:9.

[462] Zephaniah 3:9.

[463] Isaiah 11:9.

One may optionally say the following "Prayer of the Repentant":

O God, I have erred, sinned and willfully transgressed before You, and I have done that which is evil in Your eyes, especially with the sin(s) of ... (*state the specific sins or errors*).

I am sincerely ashamed of my sins, and I repent and firmly undertake not to do so again. Please God, in Your infinite grace and compassion, forgive my sins and transgressions and grant me atonement – as it is written, "Let the wicked abandon his way and the man of iniquity his thoughts; and let him return unto God, and He will show him compassion, and to our God, for He will pardon abundantly."[464] And it is written, "Do I desire at all that the wicked should die, says the Lord, God; it is rather that he return from his ways and live!"[465]

Recite Psalm 20. *(If said at other times in prayer for help, healing or delivery from trouble, say the name of the person being prayed for, even for oneself.)*

Psalms for the Seven Days of the Week
(Levites sang these in the Holy Temple in Jerusalem)

Sunday: Psalm 24   **Monday**: Psalm 48   **Tuesday**: Psalm 82
Wednesday: Psalm 94   **Thursday**: Psalm 81   **Friday**: Psalm 93
Saturday: Psalm 92 (*One may also add* Psalm 96.)

❧ Evening Prayers ❧

Recite: Psalms 91, 121 *(others may be added), and* "Lord of the universe ..."

One may say the "Prayer of the Repentant" (above) and/or Psalm 51.

Verses of placing trust in God, before sleeping (see fn. 455):

When you lie down, you will not be afraid; you will lie down and your sleep will be sweet.[466] May I sleep well; may I awake in mercy.

I entrust my spirit into Your hand; You will redeem me God, God of truth![467]

---

[464] Isaiah 55:7.
[465] Ezekiel 18:23.
[466] Proverbs 3:24.
[467] Psalms 31:6.

❧ Grace After a Meal ❧

After a person eats a satisfying amount, it is fitting for him to thank God for giving him his sustenance. It is customary to recite a prayer of "Grace" after eating a filling meal, but not after eating only a small amount. When saying "Grace After a Meal," it is proper to include thanks to God for providing other necessities – for example, health, livelihood and existence. The following two paragraphs, arranged by the author for Gentiles, are recommended (one may add further requests to God at the end, as desired):

We offer thanks to You, Master of the universe, Who in His great goodness provides sustenance for the entire world with grace, with kindness, and with mercy. He gives food to all flesh, for His kindness is everlasting. Through His great goodness to us continuously, we do not lack food, and may we never lack food, for the sake of His great Name. For He, benevolent G-d, provides nourishment and sustenance for all, does good to all, and prepares food for all His creatures whom He has created – as it is said: You open Your hand and satisfy the desire of every living thing.[468] Blessed is the God of the universe, from Whose bounty we have eaten.[469]

Please, Master of the universe, in Your mercy give us life and health, livelihood, and sustenance, so that we may thank and bless You always. Please do not make us dependent upon the gifts of mortal men nor upon their loans, but only upon Your full, open and generous hand, that we may never be shamed or disgraced. Give thanks to the Lord for He is good, for His kindness is everlasting.[470] Blessed is the man who trusts in the Lord, and the Lord will be his security.[471]

The original short Grace (as taught by Abraham to his guests):[469]
Blessed is the God of the universe, from Whose bounty we have eaten.

An alternate short Grace (especially for young children; see fn. 455):
Blessed is the Lord our God, King of the universe, Master of this bread.

---

[468] Psalms 145:16.
[469] *Midrash Rabbah Bereishit*, ch. 54. See the Preface of this book, p. 5.
[470] Psalms 136:1.
[471] Jeremiah 17:7.

Seven Verses for Noahide Children to Learn

Rabbi J. Immanuel Schochet o.b.m. recommended these verses for Noahide children to memorize and recite, especially before bedtime (with tunes):

Genesis 1:1. In the beginning God created the heavens and the earth.

Genesis 5:1. On the day that God created Adam, He made him in the image of God.

Psalms 34:15. Turn away from bad and do good; seek peace and pursue it.

Psalms 145:9. The Lord is good to all, and His mercies extend over all His works.

Proverbs 15:3. The eyes of the Lord are everywhere, seeing the bad and the good.

Job 28:28. Behold, the fear of the Lord is wisdom, and turning away from bad is understanding.

Isaiah 48:17. Thus said the Lord, your Redeemer, the Holy One of Israel: I am the Lord, your God, Who teaches you for your benefit, Who guides you in the way you should go.

Prayer for Travelers[472]

This prayer is said outside the city from which one is leaving, on the first day of the journey. On subsequent days of the journey until reaching home again, the prayer may be recited every morning.

May it be Your will, Lord our God, to lead us in peace and direct our steps in peace, to guide us in peace, to support us in peace, and to bring us to our destination in life, joy, and peace (*if one intends to return on the same day, add*: and return us in peace). Deliver us from the hands of every enemy and lurking foe, from robbers and wild beasts on the journey, and from all kinds of calamities that may come and afflict the world; and bestow blessing upon all our actions. Grant me grace, kindness, and mercy in Your eyes and in the eyes of all who behold us, and bestow bountiful kindness upon us. Hear the voice of our prayer, for You hear everyone's prayer. Blessed are You, God, Who hears prayer.

---

[472] From *Siddur Tehillat HaShem, Annotated Edition*, p. 85, pub. Kehot.

Prayer for a Sick Person

(In addition to Psalm 20 *and any other Psalms recited in prayer.)*

For a male: May the Holy One, blessed be He, be filled with mercy for (*mention the sick person's given names*), son of (*use* Noah *if the sick person is a Gentile*; *use* Sarah *if the sick person is a Jew*), to restore him to health and to cure him, to strengthen him and to invigorate him. And may God hasten to send him from Heaven a complete recovery to all his bodily parts and veins, a healing of spirit and a healing of body. Amen.

For a female: May the Holy One, blessed be He, be filled with mercy for (*mention the sick person's given names*), daughter of (*for a Gentile, use* Noah; *for a Jew, use* Sarah), to restore her to health and to cure her, to strengthen her and to invigorate her. And may God hasten to send her from Heaven a complete recovery to all her bodily parts and veins, a healing of spirit and a healing of body. Amen.

It is also appropriate to give proper charity, and to do other acts of goodness and kindness, for the sake of the healing of the sick person.

Prayer for a Newborn Gentile Baby

May God bless the woman who has given birth (*say her name, as above*), together with the child born to her (*say the child's given names*), son/daughter of (*say the father's name, as above*). May they bring him/her up to the 7 commandments, marriage and good deeds.

Prayer for a Departed Soul

May God remember the soul of (*mention the person's given names*), son/daughter of (*use* Noah *if a Gentile*; *use* Abraham *if a Jew*), who has gone on to his/her world. By virtue of my praying on his/her behalf, and, without making a vow, my intent to donate proper charity on his/her behalf, may his/her soul be bound in the Bond of Life together with the souls of the righteous, and let us say: Amen.

This may be recited (not more than once daily) during the funeral (along with Psalm 23*), memorial gathering, week of mourning, anniversary of passing, or other special occasions that are deemed appropriate. All or part of* Psalms 49 *and/or* 139 *may also be recited.*

Dedicated in memory of

Nissim ben Chasiva

Miriam bat Salcha

Avraham ben Masuda

Sara bat Adel

Made in the USA
Monee, IL
02 November 2022

70f6d05c-4e52-4508-82d5-e94d7c78f5aaR01